Tony Barrow is widely known as an international showbusiness writer with specialist knowledge of the music business since the sixties, when his career in London began as the Beatles' personal publicist between 1963 and 1968. He is editor-in-chief of Reed Midem Organisation publications associated with international music, video, multimedia and television industry programme markets. He is joint publisher and editor of an international television industry newsletter, *The Programmer* with Julian Newby.

Julian Newby is a showbusiness journalist, broadcaster and musician who works with Tony Barrow on Reed Midem Organisation publications and is joint publisher and editor of *The Programmer*. He has experience of the music business as a recording artist, a live performer, record company executive and PR consultant and has produced and presented specialist music programmes for radio. He has interviewed and written about the top names in contemporary music.

For Harvey Lee

Inside the Music Business

CAREER BUILDERS GUIDES

Inside Book Publishing
Giles Clark

Forthcoming

Inside Broadcasting

Inside the Music Business

Tony Barrow and Julian Newby

London and New York

First published 1995 by Blueprint

Reprinted 1999 by Routledge
11 New Fetter Lane, London EC4P 4EE
29 West 35th Street, New York, NY 10001

Routledge is an imprint of Taylor & Francis Group

© 1995 Tony Barrow and Julian Newby

Typeset in 10/12 Palatino by Falcon Graphic Art Ltd.
Printed in Great Britain at The Alden Press, Oxford

♾ Printed on permanent acid-free text paper, manufactured in
accordance with ANSI/NISO Z39. 48-1992 (Permanence of paper).

British Library Cataloguing in Publication Data
A catalogue record for this book is available from the British Library

Library of Congress Cataloguing in Publication Data
A catalogue record for this book is available from the Library of
Congress

ISBN 0–415–13660–1

Contents

Acknowledgements

The authors wish to thank the following for their help with this book:

Steve Alcoran
Clive Bull
The BPI
Jeremy Coopman
Jim Coulson
John Gaydon
Adrian Hopkins
Giovanna Horowitz
Jef Hanlon
Peter Hepple
IFPI
The Independent Publishers'
  Association

Dominic Jones
Josh Kirby
Debbie Lincoln
Debbie Mason
MCPS
Nick Miller
Trevor McBride
Musicians' Union
Baz O'Connel
Sharon O'Connell
RIF Raff
Nigel Rush
Chris White

Introduction

Tony Barrow

The Beatles revolutionized the recording business. There, I've said it.

I still find it hard to credit the full extent of The Beatles' impact on the machinery of the modern music industry. It's not that I have any deliberate desire to underplay the massive song-writing talents of Lennon and McCartney or to understate the innovative musical achievements of the group, but I believe I stood too close to the core of Beatlemania to be completely objective about the wider significance of the whole phenomenon, namely the direct and forceful influence which The Beatles exerted on established industrial practices. Once they became sufficiently successful to wield the necessary power, The Beatles made specific proposals and demands which led to lasting and dramatic changes in some of the traditional strategies employed by UK record companies, particularly in their relationships with artists. This all had the effect of making the music business a more comfortable workplace for the recording artists who came after them.

All those years ago in the so-called swinging sixties, I worked at the centre of the small artists' management team which surrounded The Beatles in the London headquarters of Brian Epstein's NEMS Enterprises. Between 1963 and 1968, from my unique viewpoint as the Epstein organization's in-house publicist for The Fab Four, I saw John Lennon, Paul McCartney, George Harrison and Ringo Starr learn the craft of record-making. I watched as their musical experiments threatened to outgrow the relatively lo-fi facilities of the studios where they worked. Gradually, they took control of their own recording sessions. They matured from rebellious and professionally untutored youngsters into more knowledgeable, individually ambitious and adventurous musical explorers. They didn't know it at the time, we didn't, but The Beatles were also pioneers who were rewriting the basic rule books of the music business and changing the ways in which future singers, songwriters and their bands would prepare finished product for the public. To that extent, they were at the cutting edge of an industrial evolution, some would call it revolution, which was to give the business an entirely different look and a contemporary infrastructure which we will depict and examine section by section, job by job, in the chapters of this book.

The world of music revolves around its artists – they are the shining stars and their creativity and ingenuity generate the industry's main sources of income. Music business profitability depends upon the popularity of its performers. Therefore the success of work done in many sectors of the entertainment industry depends on the artistic strength of musicians and composers, singers and bands or a combination of all four.

This book deals in some detail with the career opportunities that are available in the music business of the nineties. If you have not examined the situation until now, you may believe that all the most rewarding jobs in support of recording artists are within record companies. Some of them are, but many others are not. The skills and interests needed are wonderfully varied. Note one basic point at the outset: this book does not attempt to discuss or assess styles or standards of music. In fact it is less about music and more about the structures of the 'backstage' business set up behind the star players.

It is very possible to carve out a successful career in the music business without knowing how to compose a tune, how to sing, how to play any instrument or how to read music. Of course an interest in music helps, but the majority of job situations are not concerned with the actual making of music but with the spread of hands-on industrial activities which bring about the sale of records, music videos, concert tickets and other peripheral merchandise. Therefore it is about real people and their working lifestyles rather than faceless companies and their corporate business affairs. Without popular recording artists there would be no music business and without record companies there would be no musical product to be bought in the shops or delivered to the home. But perhaps the most essential element of all is the personnel factor. It is the people who work in the music business at a whole range of levels who are the VIPs, the celebrities, the shining stars of this book.

Some of the jobs on offer appear particularly attractive to the outsider because they provide the chance to work for or at fairly close quarters with performing artists, sometimes with well-established international superstars. If you want to get inside the music business, by all means keep some stars in your eyes and dreams in your head, but don't be fooled into thinking that the glamour and glitter of showbusiness will become any regular part of your daily routine. Some people who work closest to major artists earn relatively little money. Only the highest echelons of senior management in the music business make fortunes. Those a little lower down who make a good living often put in an awesome number of working hours compared with similarly paid executives in other lines of business. Be prepared to work very hard if you want to stay in the music business.

Although the rest of this book devotes relatively little attention to the recent history of the music business, this introductory chapter gives a valid opportunity to fill in a little background information.

If we take the introduction of weekly popular music sales charts in the UK as the beginning of a new era, it's fair to say that my generation, the teenagers of the fifties, became the first fans of modern pop music. The earliest pop chart we knew was called a Hit Parade and the first Top 20 we followed was broadcast each Sunday night by Radio Luxembourg and was based on sheet music sales data compiled by the publishing houses of London's Tin Pan Alley (Denmark Street), not on actual retail record sales.

The *New Musical Express* published a Top 12 list for the first time towards the end of 1952 and a Top 20 2 years later. When rival music papers in the consumer sector began to run their own charts, there was always the suspicion that figures were being 'cooked' to create the impression that each one was based on the most up-to-date market information – fans wanted to be first to know about the best bets for next week's number one, the latest climbers and new entries, always good topics for conversation over coffee among like-minded young friends.

Most of us heard our new releases first via crackly medium-wave transmissions from Radio Luxembourg which faded to and fro in and out of earshot. English language pop programmes were broadcast each evening from the Duchy using DJs from Britain and involving whole shows which were prerecorded in London. By the middle fifties, large brightly lit jukeboxes freshly imported from America were being installed in our local coffee bars. This pay-per-play facility gave some initial indication of a new single's sales potential, and each time someone played a new release it also acted as an extra 'plug' because others overheard it for the first time.

We bought our first singles either on 10-inch records which revolved 78 times per minute and broke if you dropped them or on the newly launched 7-inch ones which went round more slowly at only 45 revolutions per minute and did not crack as easily. The majority of pop hits played for only 2 or 3 minutes and the B-sides of singles tended to be shorter still. At home in our bedrooms, we listened to our music on record players built into austere wooden boxes with turntables which went at variable speeds at the turn of a knob. These included $33^1/3$ rpm to accommodate 10-inch and 12-inch long-players, the albums of the day, and sometimes at 16 rpm too for 'talking books'.

The output of recorded popular music in Britain came almost exclusively from a handful of so-called 'majors'. Large record companies such as Decca, EMI, Philips and Pye not only controlled home-produced product but distributed recordings made by American artists, for example Decca had the Warner and RCA labels in the UK, Philips released repertoire from the US Columbia label. The only radio station giving UK listeners a non-stop supply of pop music was Radio Luxembourg. Record companies sponsored many of the commercial station's prime-time programmes and were allowed to use them to plug new singles. On television, in the days before the Beeb introduced *Top Of The Pops*, the choice of programmes offering the record industry useful promotional opportunities for new product was exceedingly limited, Kent Walton's *Cool For Cats* on ITV and David Jacobs' *Juke Box Jury* on BBC being among the most popular.

In the fifties, it was not unusual for several British artists to record 'cover' versions of an original US hit, and two or three rival singles featuring the same song could be listed in the same week's chart.

One basic difference between the output of The Beatles in 1963 and that of their predecessors and contemporary competitors was the Liverpool group's heavy reliance upon self-composed material in an age when the singer–songwriter was a rarity. By writing their own material, The Beatles bypassed the industry's traditional full-time songwriters, the tunesmiths of Tin Pan Alley. Nor had they any need of the network of song-pluggers, the salesmen of the new songs. Song-pluggers were employees of the London music publishing houses who touted their latest tunes around the record company production departments in the hope of getting a star name or a promising new singing discovery to record some of their wares.

Prior to the meteoric rise of The Beatles during the mid-sixties, record company people, particularly the in-house producers who supervised the studio sessions, imposed their choice of raw material on recording artists. By assuming personal responsibility for the selection of their own songs, The Beatles shifted a significant amount of creative control from record company to artist. Their record producer at EMI was George Martin, who set a trend of his own by renegotiating his deal with the company and going independent. Before this, very few recordings were made by independent producers – Joe Meek, who made an extraordinary instrumental hit called Telstar with The Tornados in 1962, was an early exception, but he handed his work to Decca for release. Without the clout of such a major record company he felt it was unlikely that his single would get adequate promotion or be distributed efficiently to the retail trade around the country. It was not until the seventies that independent producers became commonplace, giving the industry a far wider spread of creative ideas than had existed during the heyday of the 'in-house' record producer. The more successful and/or prolific of the new 'indies' set up their own labels, although most still tended to use the facilities of major record companies for the machinery of manufacture, marketing and distribution.

In the fifties and sixties, the pop record market was singles led. An artist who scored with a hit single was rushed back into the studio to make an LP consisting of 10 or 12 more tracks. Inevitably, the album was given the same title as the hit single, or something very similar. The Beatles completed the recording of their first Parlophone album in 1 day of concentrated sessions, and it was named after their first chart-topping single, Please Please Me. Today the system works in reverse – an album is recorded first and then one or more singles which are taken off it for separate release are used as marketing tools – almost like the cinema industry's promotional trailer for a feature film.

Every studio recording done in the sixties was, in effect, a full-blown live performance. Artists simply rerecorded everything over and over again until the producer heard a 'take' with which he (I never came across a woman in a recording studio control room) was satisfied. It was not uncommon for this to involve up to 20 consecutive performances of the same piece by the artist, accompanied by assembled backing singers/musicians. Each studio session lasted 3 hours and was fixed like that to tie in with Musicians' Union agreements – additional recording time involved substantial extra payments to instrumentalists. As a rule, several tunes or songs were recorded at a typical 3-hour session, two for a single and maybe one left over for possible use on an LP. The Beatles broke the 3-hour three-song rule by inaugurating open-ended all-night or all-day studio sessions during which finishing touches were put to new songs prior to recording. The Beatles provided most of their own vocal and instrumental accompaniments, so session musicians were not booked on a regular basis to sit idle through these open-ended sessions but were brought in only at the moment they might be required.

The average year's engagement diary of a successful recording artist used to consist of about 10 months on the road doing concert tours and a few weeks in the recording studio. As soon as The Beatles cut short their career as stage performers in 1966 to concentrate almost exclusively on making records, they changed the established priorities completely, giving over 90% of their working time to recording sessions. This set the crucial and obviously very sensible precedent for studio time to become the most important, essential and prolonged part of a recording artist's work schedule. The era in which sessions were slotted in on occasional free days during a concert tour had come to an end.

Another industry innovation which was down to The Beatles was the pioneering of the promo video in a fairly primitive form during the second half of the sixties. It was not a device they set out to invent. The truth is that they wanted to avoid having to visit the various BBC and ITV television studios performing their new product on pop shows. Their reason for this was twofold: they were unhappy about the poor sound facilities and variable production standards and they were unwilling to do more travelling than was absolutely necessary. On the other hand, they recognized the power of television promotion and chose to begin producing their own prepackaged TV appearances in the form of short clips. This involved hiring freelance directors of their choice, shooting everything their way in their own time and distributing the finished work to broadcasters all ready to be slotted into a programme. Pop videos for television, usually financed by record companies, became a widely used promotional tool in the seventies and eighties. Dedicated music television channels of today such as MTV Music Television and Country Music Television rely almost entirely on videos as the mainstay of their programming schedules.

At the height of Beatlemania, the launching of pirate radio in Britain changed the pattern of record promotion for the music business. Rival ship-based broadcasters Radio Caroline and Radio London dominated the pirate radio scene, each competing to be the first to play new singles by top artists. PR and promotion people found they could do very simple contra deals with the pirates: if a recording artist was willing to do a personal appearance for the radio station at a club or ballroom, his or her new release would be played regularly on the air at least for a week or so. Favours of one sort or another, such as providing an early copy of a new single by a big star, were repaid by the pirates in airplay on other singles which a record company was keen to promote. At a time when there was no Radio 1 and no local radio, Caroline and London were tremendously useful to the music business in providing a playlist made up almost entirely of new product. Nor did the stations take a negative attitude about playing material by virtually unknown artists and bands; on the contrary, they enjoyed breaking a new name. The rapport between the record companies and Radio 1 was never quite so close or mutually convenient.

Two types of technological development played a big part in altering and improving the creative environment of the recording studio and its editing suites, as well as changing the way in

which songs were written, assembled and performed. One concerned the sophistication of the actual recording machinery; the
other involved the arrival of synthesizers, enabling the keyboard player's spread of instrumental sounds to became considerably broader. As new technology came to the recording studio
control room, producers who used to have an initial two or four
tracks of tape at their disposal were given a veritable superhigh-
way to play with: 16, 32 and 48 tracks upon which to put sound
from that number of different sources. This, for example, gave
the session musician a more important role in the recording
process. Retakes, whether for artistic or technical reasons, no
longer meant total reperformance of a piece but the mere drop-
ping in of single bars of music or vocal. Mixing down to make a
final master tape became an increasingly complex artistic
process which now involved the performer as well as the producer and engineer.

I have noted how artists gained some influential control of
their record-making at the expense of in-house producers. To
balance this, I should also note the eventual backlash which put
fashionable and commercially successful independent producers of the seventies and eighties in very firm control of their
recording artists. Some songwriters turned producer in order to
get their material recorded in precisely the way they wanted. To
achieve this they brought together custom-tailored groups
solely for that purpose, some consisting of session singers and
musicians who were quite unprepared for public appearances in
concert or on television. The line-up of good-looking singers
and musicians to be seen on *Top Of The Pops* or at Hammersmith
Odeon was not always the same one which had recorded the hit
single.

In parallel with the emergence of the powerful independent
producer came a proliferation of small privately owned record
companies. To service these, other independent specialists
opened recording studios and record distribution outlets.
Television advertising was used increasingly to promote
record sales both by existing record companies and by specialist new marketing firms. The newcomers concentrated on 'best
of' collections and themed album compilations containing
recordings from more than one original source. Concert tours
began to be linked more directly to album releases by timing,
title, packaging and peripheral merchandising. This was the

beginning of multimedia marketing in the music business allied to the recognition that continuity of image was very valuable in maximizing public awareness of product.

Increasingly in the eighties, as executives of the earlier days retired in the wake of mergers and restructuring, the role of the major record company shifted more emphatically towards the areas of manufacture, administration, marketing and business management. The business of recording music was left increasingly to outsiders, including a new breed of freelance producers who were also multiproduct packagers. More product was acquired in finished form from independent producers or from the small new labels with whom they had deals. At the majors, accountants and lawyers started to play more central roles, while the seeking out of new talent was left increasingly to the 'indies'. Majors today in the nineties like to think that they still do their share of talent scouting, but the fact is that a large proportion of their product is bought in, via the picking up of artists already launched successfully on independent labels or even occasionally via the outright purchase of smaller concerns.

Meanwhile, the teenagers of the fifties and sixties had matured into the middle-aged record buyers of the eighties and nineties who were prepared to upgrade their existing collections of recorded music from LP discs and analogue tape cassettes to CD. The exploitation of back-catalogue became a new priority among the majors who held the product of the fifties, sixties and seventies – the golden oldies of yesteryear began to sell all over again in CD format.

The massive technological advances which have reshaped the music business during the past three decades are continuing now in the middle nineties with new sound and video carriers coming on the market and even newer methods of direct-to-home delivery imminent.

Many of the roles played by music business employees remain virtually untouched by such radical change; others have adjusted to suit fresh circumstances. Meanwhile, each new phase of industrial evolution has increased the variety if not the overall number of opportunities available today to those who want to bring their individual and special skills to some sector of the music business. In the chapters which follow, we hope to show a comprehensive cross-section of the jobs on offer. If you choose one of these, we wish you success and professional satisfaction in a constantly changing but consistently exciting industry.

HOW TO USE THIS BOOK

The music business is essentially about selling – or earning from – copyright compositions. The processes by which these compositions get written, become published, get made into discs which in turn get sold, get played on the radio and get performed in clubs and concert halls are complex.

A successful song, its writer and its performer, will become involved with a whole range of people and companies to maximize the exploitation of their copyright. Music publishers, booking agents, concert promoters, venue managers, artists' managers, record company executives, lawyers, music journalists and radio DJs will all have a part to play at some point in the life of a successful song. Many of the people in this chain will be employed by quite separate companies. It's quite likely that a lot of them will never meet the writers or performers of any of the songs from which they indirectly earn their livings.

This book is designed to give a broad overview of the *music business* in terms of the people who work in it. One chapter will look at the role of the artists' manager, while at the same time touching upon the other people he or she might come into contact with in various working situations. Other chapters (such as the one on the artist, for example) will also touch upon the role of the manager, but each from a slightly different perspective.

Thus you, the reader, the person with an interest in becoming a part of the music business, will gain knowledge not only of many of the jobs involved, but also how they relate to each other. For example, an aspiring band manager might not have considered the extent to which managers have to deal with A&R (artist and repertoire) people, lawyers and concert promoters. Similarly, aspiring concert promoters might not have realized the extent of the financial risks involved in that profession.

This book is not intended to put off those people who yearn to enter the music business. Rather, it is designed to broaden the reader's appreciation of the business and the jobs within it – and maybe even broaden the reader's music business ambitions.

Neither is this book intended to serve as a directory of music business addresses. The list of contact addresses and phone numbers at the back exists as a first layer of contacts from which you will network out. For example, the book lists only seven major UK-based record companies. However, between them these companies own many of the country's important record labels. There are, however, a further 2000 or so record companies and labels of varying size operating in the UK. You will find a complete list in *Music Week Directory* (Appendix A).

You will also find a list of established music business-related courses at the back of this book (Appendix B). If there isn't a course for you there, i.e. there is none to suit you either academically or geographically, we advise you to get in touch with either your local education authority or the education authority in the area where you wish to live or study or both.

The industry bodies listed at the back of this book, such as the British Phonographic Industry (BPI), the International Federation of the Phonographic Industry (IFPI), the Music Publishers' Association and so on, can all provide further information and services for both those in the business and those wishing to become a part of it.

Most important to note, meanwhile, is that there is no other book available that looks at such a wide variety of jobs within the music business. We hope that, as you work through the book, you gain a clearer picture of the workings of the music business. We also hope that, if it really is your dream to join this frantic and unpredictable business, then this book will help you, in some way, to turn that dream into reality.

2

Getting inside the music business

When first considering entering the music business it's important to stop and think exactly what the term *music business* actually means. What does the music business do? The broad answer to that question is that it serves to enable and support the creation of musical *products*, such as records, videos and concerts and published musical works, for the commercial exploitation of the copyrights embodied in those products. The music business is, essentially, a rights business.

It's a somewhat cold and clinical definition, but does its job in that it serves to shatter the commonly held impression of the music business as a bunch of wacky men and women who convene on an informal basis to create music from the midst of a bohemian, good-time fog. That is not what the music business is. It is lawyers, accountants, administrators, secretaries, typists, computer programmers, agents, managers, promoters, technicians, producers, graphic designers, songwriters, song publishers, copyright agencies, musicians, singers, dancers, stage hands, drivers, box-office staff, disc jockeys, video producers and directors. It is huge, worth hundreds of millions of dollars a year, and is, in the main, not staffed by long-haired funsters who stay in bed until midday and party until the small hours, day-in and day-out.

Most of the people in the music business start work at the start of the day and go home at the end of the day. Many of them wear suits; some even wear ties. Many of them are over 40 years old and some much older! Most of them couldn't play a musical instrument to save their lives, don't mix with the stars and don't take drugs.

Are you put off yet? If you're truly keen on entering the music business, none of the above will have dissuaded you because, while much of the music business operates just like any other, there are things that make it special.

WHAT'S SO SPECIAL ABOUT THE MUSIC BUSINESS?

Who invented the game of Monopoly? Who designed the Austin Mini? Who was the creator of *Star Trek*? Who wrote (most of) The Beatles' songs? Name at least one of the Jackson family. Pose these five questions about popular culture to any group of people over the age of 18 and you'll find that, while many will struggle with the first three, pretty well anyone and everyone will know the answer to the last two. That's what's so special about the music business; whatever colour, race, creed or nationality, most people will have been touched by its product in some way at some time in their lives.

To be involved in some aspect of the creative process which results in the creation of that product and all the romance, glamour and excitement which might surround it at any given time is what attracts most people to the music business. The purpose of this book is to explain the various roles to which those people might best be suited, and how and where they fit into the business

WHO MAKES UP THE MUSIC BUSINESS?

It is typical for those people who are keen to 'get into the music business' to presume that contacting a record company might be their logical starting point. Not necessarily. Taking the UK as an example, of the 48 600 or so people who work in the music business, only 7900 are employed by record companies (source: BPI surveys and estimates for 1992). That figure is divided roughly 50:50 between manufacturing and distribution (4100) and record company administration and marketing (3800).

The remaining 40 700 are employed as follows: retailing (14 500); professional musicians (8000); service and support industries (3800); journalism and publishing (2500); composers and songwriters (2500); recording studios (2000); music publishing (2000); broadcasting and video production (2000); entertainment venues (1900), and recording equipment manufacture (1500).

As the figures show, to limit yourself to just the record companies when making your first attempts at entering the music business is to ignore some 80% of the industry and, therefore, 80% of any music business jobs that might be going.

Considering the above statistical breakdown, it would be worth spending some time working out exactly what it is about the music business that appeals to you before you start writing letters, making phone calls and knocking on doors.

WHICH JOB?

What is it that you really want to do? Are you a musician? If so, you will already know what sort of music you like to play and, if you're serious, will be preparing for the months and even years of low pay, heartache and sheer hard slog which have to be gone through before you can be certain of being able to make a living from your talent. Chapters 16 to 20 in this book deal with the long and winding road to success that all artists have to tread and, more importantly, those moments of joy all artists experience at those times when their craft is satisfactorily executed and/or warmly appreciated by others.

Writers and composers provide the raw materials, yet need not endure any of the hard slog and drudgery which can go hand in hand with live performance and record promotion generally. Writers and composers can have a tough time breaking into the business and, on the rock and pop side, tend to find that performing their own material is the best way of getting it heard. As is explained later in this book, however, the songwriter who wins a publishing deal without needing to perform, and whose songs are in demand from top-selling artists, can claim to have the best of all worlds. It is also important to remember that the rights to those songs are, in the end, what the music business is all about. Owned by songwriters, record companies and publishers, it is the royalties paid on these rights which essentially fuel the whole business.

Maybe management is your forte and you wish to apply these skills to the music business rather than any other simply because you happen to like music. But do you like musicians? If you don't know the answer to that question, then maybe you should try to find out. Chapter 4 looks at the rewards the artist management business has to offer, and also warns of the problems managers might face in the execution of their duty. Many a manager has sat back stage or in the studio control room, head in hands, asking the question: 'Why didn't I go into office management, bank management or even supermarket management? Anything but this!' But then there are others – those whose artist or artists have made it big – who are now enjoying both the way of life and the 20%.

As the statistics show, retailing is the biggest and, in many ways, the most important sector of the music industry. Yet, ironically, it is probably the easiest of all to get into. That is because, at the lowest level, a specialist musical knowledge is not always required. Personability, personal presentation, efficiency, honesty and basic numeracy are important qualities in all retailing, and if you have those qualities then there's no reason why a record retailer should reject you any more than a book or clothes retailer might. That said, if you show knowledge of and an enthusiasm for the music industry once you've been successful in getting work in the record retail business, the opportunities to sidestep into other areas of the music business do exist.

A natural sideways movement from retailing is into A&R. These two initials stand for *artist* and *repertoire*, the A&R man or woman being the person responsible for the 'discovery' of new talent and the subsequent guidance of that talent through the business of signing to a record label. The A&R department of a record company will also be involved in decisions concerning the material – or repertoire – to be performed, recorded and released by the artist. Retail provides a good grounding for A&R because the retailer is at the sharp end of the industry, taking money from fans and enthusiasts who are, after all, the people who decide the fate of all artists. An A&R person must also have a passion for the live gig as this is where most talent is discovered and where an audience reaction can be instantly gauged.

THE SUPPORT SYSTEMS

We've talked so far about the sharp-end jobs – the composers, the artists, the people who discover and manage those artists and the people who actually hand over the finished product to the record-buying public at the counter. Working alongside all these people are those who support the creation and subsequent exploitation of musical product through providing technical, legal, financial and related services.

Excluding the comparatively new breed of artist–producers, producers rank among the unsung heroes of the music business. They are usually well paid (if they enjoy reasonable success) but very much in the background as far as the public face of the business is concerned. The job is a crucial one, however, for it is the producer who both interprets the material for recording and, in collaboration with the studio engineer (another unsung hero), oversees the recording process through from composition to the finished product. Many producers also take on the job of seeking out the right songs for their artists, as well as choosing the musicians. The job of producer is the logical step up from that of studio engineer, which is a job requiring a high level of technical expertise combined with strong musical instincts, although there are other routes to this most prestigious of jobs.

Another behind-the-scenes job is that of the publisher. Songwriters and composers who sign their rights over to a publisher get a very strange service in return. The publisher's job is to get a writer's material used – by live performers, recording artists and commercials, film and television producers, and manage the resulting earnings. Publishers will sometimes provide the resources to enable writers to nurture their talent; in the case of performer–songwriters, they will often contribute to the financing of tours, studio time, publicity material and so on. The publisher will control the copyright and negotiate royalties on an artist's behalf.

The ultimate goal of many publishers is to own a catalogue of properties which earn money by themselves – music which is in such demand by radio stations, television channels, film producers and performers that all the publisher has to do is sit back and watch those percentages come rolling in. Of course, no publisher will admit to practising the profession in such a way, but it is this perception which has long tainted the image of the publishing business. Should you decide that publishing is for you, you will soon become aware of this image some others in the industry have of the publisher. However, to work in music publishing requires considerable negotiating skills and knowledge of the workings of copyright law and of the music business generally, all of which are hard to acquire outside the music publishing business itself.

THE MEN IN SUITS

If publishers have a bad reputation within some quarters of the music business, compared with that of the music lawyer the publisher's reputation is whiter than white. The commonly held view is that lawyers are disliked or at least mistrusted from within the music business. Artists resent them for putting legal and financial considerations over creative and artistic ones, and record companies resent them for standing between them and the artists in whom they're investing so much money. Like it or not, however, lawyers are crucial to a business which is now truly international, and in which there is so much money to be made and lost. And as the music industry slowly becomes more of a multimedia industry, so lawyers will become increasingly more important to the task of determining who owns what element of a production and how much it's worth.

In some areas of the business, concert promoters and agents suffer a reputation similar to those of the publishers and lawyers – as people who sponge off the creative efforts of others, doing little more that sitting back and taking their percentage while others do all the hard work. But that's just one side of the equation. Along with the job of promoting a live band there is considerable risk. The promoter must know what makes a good live act, must be able to fit the act to the venue, must coordinate equipment and personnel so that the concert happens when it is supposed to happen; and, most of all, the promoter must get the sums right so that everyone who requires payment actually does get paid.

THE HARD SELL

One area of the music business which many artists in the past used to ignore altogether is that of marketing. Back in the late sixties, when rock music was going through its 'progressive' period, many artists were insisting that their music should speak for itself and so were denying interviews to the press, radio and television and generally refusing to take part in activities which are today regarded as crucial to the successful marketing of a band or record. Some bands, notably Led Zeppelin, were even refusing to make singles, which today exist almost solely as marketing tools for albums.

Today almost every aspect of artists and their product is considered when a marketing strategy is being planned – from what artists wear to where they're seen in public. The video, the TV advertisement, radio airplay, the packaging of the record and the timing of the release are all carefully considered so that the record hits the shops with maximum impact. Many artists object to the demands made on them by the marketing department of the record company, and some even feel that the hard sell denigrates their work. Nonetheless, it is a crucial element of today's music business and it employs a large number of people. Marketing is an area in which many training opportunities exist, and general training combined with a passion for and a broad knowledge of music would stand anyone in good stead for a career in this area of the business.

GETTING INSIDE

The above summary of the music business covers key roles but not every role. DJs, fan clubs and merchandising, public relations, video production, session musicians, roadies and others crucial to the business have yet to be discussed. What this chapter hopefully will have done, though, is provided a context within which you can begin to work out where you will fit into this complex and varied business.

The music business has always been about relationships: what you know is often less important than who you know and where you came from and, in spite of the fact that it has become so much more of a business and so much less of a creative free-for-all, music industry career paths remain hard to find and badly maintained. There are few formal qualifications which will ensure you a job, and even today few career guidance professionals place the music business high on their list of priorities. We will discuss formal routes into the business later, but at this stage it is important to know that without commitment, determination and enthusiasm, and access to a fairly thick skin when needed, no attempt at entering the business will succeed in the long term.

3

The record company

Contrary to the thinking of most people, record companies do not constitute the main element of the music industry. In fact, even if we were to include manufacturing and distribution as part of the work done by a record company (and most record companies farm out these activities, majors excepted) then still the record companies employ only 7900 of the total 48 600 people working in the business (Chapter 2).

To put the record company as we know it into some sort of context, it would be beneficial to consider life before the record company, and how it eventually came into being.

THE INTRODUCTION OF COPYRIGHT

We could go back many hundreds and even thousands of years before we might find the first person ever to make money from performing his or her own piece of music. Yet it was only a couple of hundred years ago that music actually started to be published. Before that time, the means by which someone could *own* the rights to a piece of music, and thus insist on payment from anyone else wishing to *use* that piece of music, simply didn't exist.

From the wandering minstrel to music hall artist, from the court musician to Mozart, people have been paid for singing and playing for centuries. In the case of the latter it was as much the music as the person that people were paying for, although it was only ever the actual *performance* for which people were being asked to pay. Money would otherwise come from commissions, royalty or aristocracy requesting the creation of a piece of music for a particular event and paying generously for it.

The introduction of the concept of copyright was really what turned music into a true *business*. Music copyright was introduced to protect its creators. The first music publishers (Chapter 5) were given the job of publishing songwriters' or composers' work in the form of sheet music, registering the copyright and collecting the payments from anyone who used that music for personal financial gain. The publisher would then take a cut before paying the creator a *royalty*. Once recording became commonplace, so the protection and exploitation of this copyright became a more complex and lucrative business. The record companies came into being in order to organize, carry out and develop this business.

THE MODERN RECORD COMPANY

Record companies have changed considerably since they came into being with the arrival of the recordable cylinder back in the late nineteenth century. The most noticeable change over the last 15–20 years is that they have become increasingly like proper businesses, in other words run to make a profit by people who know how to make a profit rather than by people who simply love or enjoy music. This is, in fact, the cause of one of the biggest criticisms levelled at record companies and the music business as a whole these days – that it is now run by faceless accountants in grey suits rather than people who know and care about the artists and their creations.

There is some truth in this, although it would be crazy to suggest that record companies and the industry generally could do without people with a passion for music. Likewise it would be crazy to suggest that such companies, particularly of the size to which many have grown in recent years, could stay afloat without a network of lawyers, accountants, managers and directors. However, before you decide upon a career with a record company, it would be as well to note that these days most of them are run like any other company.

TYPES OF RECORD COMPANY

There are three broad types of record company. The smallest is the privately owned or independent record company or, in music business jargon, the indie. Indies are usually set up to work in a specialist area of the business.

The second type can be described as an *indie within a major*, that is to say a company which looks and acts like an indie but which is actually a subsidiary of a major. Such a record company, or *label*, has the best of both worlds in the sense that it enjoys the intimacy and identity of an indie, while at the same time enjoying the muscle and financial security afforded to it by its parent major.

The third and biggest type of record company is the aforementioned *major*. Major record companies are usually multinationals, or part of a multinational, such as Sony or EMI, which are *vertically integrated* in that they all operate their own publishing manufacturing and distribution operations. Increasingly, the multinationals are stretching that level of vertical integration, by taking control of the hardware as well as the software industries. (Sony, originally a hardware manufacturer, now owns what was CBS Records, which was formed in 1938, and its sister company Epic Records, formed 20 years later – see below.)

An even more recent development has seen the majors controlling radio stations.

The indie

An indie could be run from a small bedroom. All that's really needed is a phone, preferably something to put it on, someone to answer it and an answerphone to replace that person when he or she is out. A small amount of capital is also required. In the early days of such a *bedroom operation* few get paid, the exceptions being those people and organizations which provide services such as cab companies, phone companies, stationery wholesalers, CD manufacturers, recording studios, etc.

An indie usually starts with an artist or group of artists, a bunch of songs and the ability and desire on the part of one or more people to record them. Let's take the example of one which operates on behalf of just one band. First you take song and band into a studio and record. (This might be done before or after a publishing deal is sought and signed – Chapter 5.) Most reasonable-sized towns have one or two recording studios, some better than others, and most will provide the services of an engineer. You would probably produce the recording yourself (Chapter 8), at the same time taking the technical advice of the engineer. Apart from instruments, this recording will be your first major expense. (A band's instruments also constitute a major expense, but most members will have already sold all but the clothes they stand up in to buy these so they don't count in the initial outlay – except, of course, when you're preparing your accounts for the Inland Revenue, when they will count as capital input.)

If at first you're only planning a single or EP (3–6 tracks) you are only likely to need a couple of days of studio time, which is unlikely to cost you more than a few hundred pounds.

Your recording then has to be mixed down from the multitrack master tape to a quarter-inch analogue tape, a half-inch high-speed analogue tape or, most common these days, a digital audio tape (DAT) master (more cost). It is from this that your records – or tapes, if you really are a small, low-budget operation – will be pressed (if you're making vinyl records) or duplicated (if you're a tape-only operation – the cheapest route). This master you take to a pressing plant, which will press any number of records you request – major cost number three. Most plants will press a minimum of 500. The more you have pressed, the lower the cost per disc. Then there are labels and packaging to be considered. These actually constitute a fairly small proportion of the total manufacturing cost but have to be planned carefully, as with such a low-budget exercise they will play a large part in the branding of both the act and your company.

The brokerage

There are companies, called brokerages, which will take your DAT master and organize all the above for you, from the pressing of the record to the design and printing of the labels and covers and packaging of the product. Such brokerages can often save you money as they benefit from certain economies of scale. The pressing plant or even the studio you use will be able to put you in touch with a brokerage. The studio or plant might even have business links with a brokerage.

CD or vinyl?

The process we have briefly described above, which has your multitrack master mixed on to DAT before going to a pressing plant, applies to vinyl discs. The vinyl manufacturing process involves the signals on the DAT being converted into electronic impulses which cause a stylus to vibrate and cut grooves into an aluminium disc coated with lacquer. This then goes through two more processes before a positive stamper is created which is used to make the negative imprints onto vinyl blanks, which in turn become your records.

If you intend to release your recording on CD, the process will be slightly different. In the case of CD your master will have to be on digital tape – with vinyl, masters can be created from quarter-inch analogue tape. Most studios now use only digital tape, and this is then used to prepare the *glass master* from which a series of *stampers* is created. The discs are produced by forcing plastic into a mould in which the stamper sits. The discs are then metallized to make them reflective and finally coated with a lacquer and printed with the label.

Which do you go for, CD or vinyl? Well, if you're seriously hoping for this record to be mass marketed, then you will have to go for CD and possibly both. If, on the other hand, this is a record aimed at club DJs, you'll want it manufactured in the form of a 12" single.

Cassettes

The cheapest way of all to mass produce recordings is by copying or *dubbing* off the master on to a series of cassettes. If you have the time and a decent tape-to-tape machine (or series of machines), and your budget and your initial run are low, you can do this yourself. It will take a lot of time, but will save you some money. There are also *duplication houses* with the equipment to run off hundreds and even thousands of cassettes for you at very high speed. If you do decide to use one of these, shop around because there is a lot of competition in this field. Bear in mind though that a cheap duplication house might be using cheap tape and cheap equipment, which will make your recording sound cheap. Personal recommendation will help you here.

Even if you're not at the stage where your records are ready for the mass market, cassettes of your songs will often sell well at gigs, and there is often more money to be made in this way than from your gig fee, which will probably be negligible.

Selling the records

Then the product has to be marketed and distributed. Marketing may be done by you – by flyposting (sticking posters up at key places around the town/country, usually an illegal practice but very common nonetheless), leafleting venues, colleges, wherever you feel your market is, begging for press and radio coverage and by taking out advertisements if your budget stretches to this. The key element in your marketing campaign (Chapter 9) is to persuade the retailer that it's worth stocking your band's record. If your band is known to a retailer, through local reputation for example, then you have no problem. If your band is unknown, then that's where skilled marketing becomes essential, and part of this job will be done by the distributor.

For distribution you will need to strike a deal with one of the well-known independent distribution companies – or possibly, though less likely at the early stages, by the distribution arm of a major. Distribution companies exist simply to get other people's records into the shops and are usually servicing many different labels at the same time. If you do intend to strike a deal with a distributor – and a distributor will only take your product if it sees that it is going to be properly promoted and thinks it will sell – the deal will see the distributor taking just under 30% of the dealer price, rather than the retail price, of the record. Some distributors will offer the services of a brokerage.

Then the record must be plugged (Chapter 12). Exposure on radio and television is still the best means of promoting a record. To get a record on to a radio playlist is one of the toughest tasks facing anyone in the music business. Moreover, unless your band has a very interesting story behind it that appeals, for whatever reason, national television is most times out of the question in the UK.

Local press is usually very accommodating to new local enterprises; national press will always want an angle (usually sexual, criminal or celebrity related) and the music press will usually only ever write about a new act if it forms part of a *happening trend*, or if the publication feels its profile will be well served by appearing to have discovered this new act. So, you should tailor your press campaign accordingly (Chapter 11).

So an indie is born. If your first few efforts reap rewards, offices and staff can then be paid for.

How distribution works

Whether distribution is in-house (as with a major) or farmed out to an independent distributor as would happen with an indie, the process is largely the same in both cases.

Taking the case of an album set for release by your own indie, you will have to approach the distributor yourself. The distributor will first want to know how the record is to be promoted, the history of the band and other details, such as the date you want the record released, the price you're selling the record to the dealer (this will usually be standard), the catalogue number of the release and so on. The distributor will then want promotional copies of the record to take to the head offices of all the major record retail chains to discuss in-store promotion and other methods by which the record might be promoted. Then, the distributor's sales representatives go out and pre-sell the record to the stores and take pre-sale orders from the retailers. Pre-sales will determine how many copies you, the record label, should have pressed (unless you or they know that the record will sell well) and a good distributor will advise you on this. Then, 1 week before the release date, the distributor will place its order with you and its vans will then pick up the records and deliver them to the shops.

The structure of a major

Where a major will differ fundamentally from an indie is that most of the services required to turn a song into a mass-marketable item exist within the structure of the company itself. The other key difference between an indie and a major is that an indie, although always seeking to grow and develop, will usually retain an identity based on a core of artists of a particular genre, while a major will cast its net ever wider for new artists, and will comprise a series of labels to which artists are signed, depending upon where their musical style fits into the marketplace as a whole.

A major will also differ from an indie in the sense that majors today are multinationals, and therefore have outlets for their product worldwide. Indies, on the other hand, will license their product to other labels overseas in order to sell their artists abroad. In other words, the licensor will allow the licensee to manufacture records from the master provided by the licensor. The licensee will then sell and market the record in its territory (usually in collaboration with the licensor's production, sales and marketing departments) in return for a percentage paid to the licensor.

In this chapter we have given the simplest example of how an independent record company can be set up and run. It would be impossible, after all, to describe the typical indie – just as it would be to describe the typical major. We can, however, look at the various departments common to most majors, so as to be able to understand better how such an integrated operation runs. (Some of the points discussed below could apply to both a large indie and an *indie within a major*.)

The board

Most large record companies have a board of directors with a managing director, chairperson or president responsible to the board for the running of the company. Directors on the board may be employed by the company or simply representatives of major shareholders. If they are employed by the company they might also head a number of the company's departments.

The A&R department

If a record company is primarily in the business of selling recorded music, then the artists and repertoire (A&R) department, under the A&R manager, is the key to the whole operation.

The job of the A&R manager and staff is, essentially, to find the music and the artists – the record company's raw materials. A&R people will first, by a number of means at their disposal, *discover* the new talent and then apply their skills to the job of persuading that talent to sign up with the record company.

It is then the A&R department's job to negotiate the record deal, along with a number of other professionals within the company, including lawyers and accountants and possibly the managing director or somebody who reports directly to that person. Recording and promotion of artist will follow and A&R will oversee this too. So, as far as work on the creative side of a record company is concerned, A&R is about as hands-on as you'll get.

The marketing department

In between A&R and production sits the marketing department. This could exist in the form of a single employee, or even an independent, contracted company, depending on the size of the record company or project. The marketing department (Chapter 9) will, in collaboration with A&R, artist management and possibly board members, arrange and coordinate advertising schedules across a number of media, as well as coordinate press and promotions campaigns and visibility at retail outlets. Press and promotions will, in most cases, be coordinated by a separate publicity department in collaboration with marketing.

The creative services department

Working closely with production and marketing, this department will coordinate sleeve, poster and advertisement design, sometimes set design for larger concert tours and occasionally get involved in video production (Chapter 10). In smaller record companies, or with particularly big artists, this work might be contracted out to an independent design or marketing company.

The production department

The term production here does not refer to the production of a record (Chapter 8). Rather, it refers to all that needs to be done to ensure that the records are manufactured, packaged and released on time. The production department, under the product manager, will work closely with A&R to ensure that the mastering and then the pressing of a record go according to schedule and will also ensure that the production and delivery of sleeves, labels, records, cassettes and CDs happens in accordance with the proposed release date.

Stock control, sometimes a separate department altogether,

often forms part of the production department. The production department, in constant contact with distribution, will inform stock control of the number of records to be produced and it is then stock control's responsibility, in collaboration with the sales force, to see that stock doesn't go unsold, or that demand is always fulfilled. A record left on the shelf of a record store loses money, as does an out-of-stock title that is still being requested by customers.

The sales and distribution department

The principal job of the sales and distribution workforce is to take orders from retailers and supply records, along with promotional material such as stickers, t-shirts and posters, to those retailers, and in sufficient numbers. With new artists, extra promotional work will be required and *strike forces* will, in such cases, be sent out to target specific retailers, particularly those known for their ability and willingness to promote new acts. Once an artist is known, or a particular title is doing well, the job of the sales and distribution department is to ensure that shops always have enough records to sell.

The very large record companies will have their own manufacturing plants too. The sales and distribution and production departments will be constantly in touch with manufacturers via the production department. Manufacturers then release product to the distribution warehouses. The sales force then takes the product on to the retailer. The timing of these two stages is crucial to the potential success of a release. This is because the marketing of a record, which might involve a poster campaign, a media campaign (including TV appearances of the act in question, pictures and interviews in the music press, etc.), press, radio and television advertising, has to be planned well in advance. If the record which is being marketed isn't available for retailers at the time when the artist is enjoying all this publicity, then sales will be lost.

The international department

No artist makes really big money in the record business unless he or she *breaks* in more than one *territory*. The term territory usually means *country*, but in certain circumstances can mean a group of countries in which trends follow similar paths. In record marketing terms, The US is a territory; Australia and New Zealand together make up a single territory, as do Germany, The Netherlands and Belgium. Scandinavia, too, is regarded as a single territory. The head of the international department – perhaps this is the international director who might also sit on the board – has the job of identifying the right territory or territories for a particular product and negotiating for its release there. This is usually done by way of a licensing agreement, the domestic record company being the licensor and the foreign company the licensee (see below). However, if we're talking about a multinational with offices around the world, then the international strategy for a release becomes a whole lot simpler.

Along with this, worldwide publicity campaigns and tours have to be organized and coordinated with release dates, a hugely complex and time-consuming business, but worthwhile when you consider that for a UK artist selling a record worldwide could multiply income 10-fold, as the UK industry represents somewhere in the region of 10% of that of the whole world.

The licensing agreement

For small independent record companies without operations overseas, it is through licensing agreements that their records are released abroad. A licensing agreement is where one record company (the licensor) allows another (the licensee) to produce copies from a master supplied by the original record company.

As part of the agreement, the licensor will make certain demands of the licensee, for example that the licensee will adopt a marketing strategy approved by the licensor, that it will only release the record under the strict terms outlined in the agreement, that certain quality controls will be applied to the release, and so on.

Licensing agreements are also often made between companies operating in the same country. Many *compilation* albums of hits are put together by a licensee having acquired the licence to reproduce masters of particular recordings from a string of licensors. In such cases, the recorded songs in question are usually those which have passed their *sell by date* as singles but which would have value when included on a themed compilation album.

THE MAJOR AND THE ARTIST

The relationship between the major record company and the artist is becoming increasingly problematic, as has been clearly demonstrated by the long drawn-out court case between George Michael and Sony. The case was a complicated one and was watched with a mixture of fascination and trepidation by everyone in the music business. 'Could the lone artist stand up to a multinational the size of Japan's Sony Corporation?' was the question on everyone's lips. And the eventual answer was 'no'.

Part of the reason why the court case came about in the first place was that during the course of his career, in spite of his growing in stature as a star, George Michael had become a smaller part of a rapidly growing empire. His old group Wham! had signed to Epic Records, the sister label of 50-year-old major CBS. Although under the CBS umbrella, 30-year-old Epic operated as a separate label, and had its own identity. When Sony bought CBS in 1988, things began to change. Minor corporate adjustments made by the bosses in Japan often seemed like sweeping changes to those working at Epic or CBS in London, and so many working within these newly bought record companies, artists included, began to feel like shrinking cogs in a wheel that was growing in size by the minute.

Such corporate changes are happening all the time. In the summer of 1993, PolyGram, which owns a diverse collection of record companies including Island (formerly the indie fortress of renowned record entrepreneur Chris Blackwell) and A&M (the 'A' of which stands for Alpert, as in Tijuana trumpeter Herb Alpert), bought the legendary Motown record company. This move has put Diana Ross under the same roof as Placido Domingo. Almost gone are the days when a record company's identity was determined by the type of artist it signed.

WORKING FOR A RECORD COMPANY

Clearly, working for an indie will be totally different from working for a major. A reasonable-sized indie will be split into some of the departments listed above, but in many cases if you're working for a small indie you are likely to find that many jobs cross over. For this reason, an indie can serve as the perfect training ground for a future in one of the majors, as while working for an indie you will have touched upon all aspects of the business. Within an indie you will begin to decide which area you want to specialize in and hopefully concentrate your efforts in that direction. This experience can then be taken to a major, where you will be able to join the particular department which will benefit best from your acquired experience and ambition.

Record company structures vary from country to country, but the processes described – signing a band, developing the material, recording the material, packaging the material, promoting the material and finally getting the material into the shops – are the same all over the world.

4

Artist management

The artist's manager is a much-maligned figure in the music business. The manager takes too much from the artist; drives too hard a bargain with the record company; earns a percentage even when the income has been derived from an activity in which he or she has had no involvement whatsoever; and enjoys all the fun, the glamour, the money, but doesn't have to sell his or her soul on stage night after night or burn out in the studio for months on end.

What does a manager do anyway? At the very least, an artist's manager does everything the artist cannot or will not do in terms of planning, organization and negotiation. And if the person in question is an effective, creative manager, he or she will do a lot more besides.

Before moving on to answer that question in detail, however, a word of warning: if everyone who'd been asked to manage a singer, songwriter or band had taken up the challenge, there would be an awful lot of discarded, dejected and even bankrupt ex-managers wandering the streets looking for work. Many of them would be sporting black eyes, broken arms and legs and possibly worse. It is a trap so many artists and their friends fall into. The authors of this book couldn't put a figure on the number of times they themselves have been asked to manage this band or that singer. So many artists reach that stage in their careers (usually while they're still amateur) at which either their egos or the level of activity they have reached tell them they need, or think they need, a manager. And usually the first person they approach is a brother, a sister, or a close friend of the band. Quite what is going through their minds when they make such a proposition is difficult to say. In some cases it's simply that they feel that there's a certain prestige attached to having a manager; in other cases it's simply that they don't want the responsibility of organizing things any more, and would prefer to be getting on with the 'serious, creative' business of writing and performing.

Should you be tempted to accept such an offer, it's important that you first ask yourself the following questions:

- Why did they ask *you*?

- Do you sincerely believe this artist/band has a *future*? Do you like and believe in what they do?

- Do you have the *time* to dedicate to the task?

- Does this artist/band make any *money*? If so, are they likely to agree to *pay* you a percentage of that money on a regular basis? And if not, who's going to pay for your time, your phone bill and your petrol until the money does start coming in?

- Are these people *good friends*? If so, is it worth risking that friendship, bearing in mind that artist–management relationships can go badly wrong? Offending someone by saying no will likely cause you fewer problems than were you to take on the task only to suffer an acrimonious fall-out later on.

- Do you have any *experience* – either in showbusiness, a record company or in general management? If not, might it be wise to go off and get some and hope the manager's job will still be there when you get back?

- Do you really *want* to be an artist manager? It is a full-time job, not a part-time job, and other interests, inside or outside the music business, are likely to suffer if you it take on.

All the above serves to reinforce the point that effective management requires more than a mere respect or affection for the artist or artists concerned. To manage a successful band is a tough task, and requires skills which are best learned through either experience or training or, ideally, both. Should you ever find yourself in the position where somebody is asking you, even begging you, to manage them, make sure you can first provide satisfactory answers to all the above, and then think through a list of music's more successful, high-profile managers: John Reid, long-time manager of Elton John; Ed Bicknell, manager of Dire Straits; Miles Copeland, manager of Sting; Bill Drummond, former manager of Echo And The Bunnymen, and later of KLF; Paul McGuinness, manager of U2; Malcolm McLaren, manager of The Sex Pistols. What do they all have in common? Answer: charisma, aggressive drive and a healthy 'don't give a stuff' attitude to what the industry, the public, and sometimes even their artists, think of them. Is that you? If not, you are advised to think again.

And still bearing the above list in mind, ask yourself this question: how is the success of these people defined? Would they have turned out to be successful managers had not their clients themselves had exceptional talent? A point worth remembering: a manager can only be a success if the artist or artists he or she manages are a success. Whether or not a manager can *create* a successful artist is a debate to which there is probably no end.

It is important to keep reminding yourself that, while managers should believe in their artists both creatively and commercially, they don't necessarily need to have too much else in common with them. Friendship helps and respect is important, but like-mindedness is not essential, and is in fact quite rare between artist and manager. When asked once how he reconciled his political views with those of his very right-wing manager, Sting replied: 'I may not agree with his views, but I'd die for his right to express them'. Now there's a perfect artist–manager relationship: the artist retains his integrity while the manager deals with all the tough, unpleasant stuff behind the scenes.

WHEN AND WHY IS A MANAGER REQUIRED?

Let us take a look at the manager's job from the artist's perspective for a moment. A band has been together for a few months, maybe over a year, and has reached the stage where a demo tape is required to further its fortunes. This demo could be home-produced or, if the money's there, put together in a professional studio. The band's next step is to tout that recording around – to venues in order to get more and better live work, and to record companies, presuming that what the band's ultimately after is a record deal. Does this band have the time, the ambition and, most important, the talent and the right business approach to use that demo in the most effective way possible? They may be great writers and performers, but are they salespeople too? If the answer to those two questions is 'no', and the band members are totally dedicated to the project and the music, then this is one stage in a band's career where a manager could mean the difference between success and failure.

Switching back to the manager's point of view: if you are serious about a career in artist management, you should now step back and consider at what point in a band's or an artist's career you should be taking control. The story of the manager who took a band up to the point at which they were about to take off and then dumped them, or was dumped by them, is far too common. For the definitive story, read the hugely entertaining book *The Man Who Gave The Beatles Away* by Allan Williams. Along with The Beatles' first drummer and the A&R man at Decca who turned The Beatles down, Williams ranks among the three most unlucky men in rock and roll. True, one could, and many do, argue that The Beatles would never have enjoyed the sort of success under Williams (or any other manager for that matter) that they did under Brian Epstein, who had a particular passion for the band; but Williams' tale is a salutary one nonetheless.

Back to the artist or band with the freshly recorded demo. Its members have decided they need a manager. They now face three broad choices: enlisting the services of a friend, colleague or associate with some interest in the band (a scenario already dealt with earlier), self-management or approaching a management company.

SELF-MANAGEMENT

Yes, it can be done, and is done by more and more artists these days, particularly those in the club field who write, record and produce tracks, often anonymously, and distribute them cottage industry style to DJs and specialist shops. Such people are often driven as much by entrepreneurial aspirations as musical ones, and in such cases self-management makes a lot of sense. There are also those acts which are as much businesses as they are sources of entertainment, such as Soul II Soul, which is not just a band but also a retail and merchandising company. Such 'verti-cally integrated' outfits often have their own business infra-structure and, as such, don't require a manager in the traditional sense.

Self-management can also make sense to a solo singer–song-writer and even a traditional four- or five-piece band. Signing a management deal with a third party too early can cause prob-lems – both now, when there's little or no money being made, and later if and when the money does start coming in and the original agreement begins to look iniquitous to either or both parties. It is not uncommon for bad management deals to res-onate years after a band has split with its management and the members have even split with each other. A deal gone really badly wrong can ruin careers for good. So self-management in the early days might serve some artists well. And should they manage to achieve a certain level of acclaim – and, more impor-tantly, earnings – in this way, they will be better placed to sign the right management deal when the time comes for them to hand the job over to someone else.

Self-management does require artists to look at their business affairs separately from the creative and performance side of their work, in other words to see their artistic side as purely a revenue-earning activity, and many will find this hard to do. However, an artist with a clear business head plus the assistance of lawyers and accountants when required can do well in the manager's role. Diana Ross is one such artist. So you see, it can work.

THE MANAGEMENT COMPANY

There are lone managers, those who perhaps accepted an offer from a friend or friends as they were struggling towards suc-cess, or those who were wooed by artists from their safe job within a record company; and there are those who work within the more secure confines of a management company.

A job with a reputable management company could well serve as a good start for a number of different careers in the music business, but you're advised to choose your company with care. There are known sharks in the music management business, and while we don't wish to put across the message that music management is at all a questionable profession, for that is not necessarily the case, it would be worth your while sounding out any music business contacts you may have before considering a post with any management company.

Where a management company can prove more effective than the lone manager is in economies of scale. An established company will have premises for a start, plus secretarial and other administrative staff, possibly legal and financial staff and, most importantly, a number of managers whose combined experience will serve all clients, whichever individual manager within the company may deal with them personally.

Taking a junior position with a management company, as office assistant or even messenger, would allow you to watch the business at work with the purpose of acquiring expertise and/or deciding whether management was really for you. The qualifications required to join such a company can vary; and as you will read over and over again in this book, you'll stand the best chance if someone within the company knows you or knows of you, or vice versa.

A keenness to learn must be demonstrated too. If you have acquired some form of management training and are able to prove to a management company that you have a love of, and active interest in, music and the music business, and you're bright and personable too, then it would be a foolish management company that didn't take you on.

Artist management companies are often partnerships, formed to combine the management experiences and expertise of two or more people and at the same time to cut costs by sharing overheads. To get into such a company at anything other than administrative level would be tough, but things move fast in the music business, and a good administrative assistant within a management company would be well placed to move into management if this was his or her goal.

Another route to management is via a record company. Many managers come across their clients while working for a record company – as an A&R person or press officer for example. In such cases, close relationships can build up between the artist and record company staff, sometimes to the point at which the artist finally makes the formal request for the staff member concerned to become his or her manager. This can often be the ideal situation, because a working relationship has already been established. If, however, the would-be manager in this case leaves the record company and goes it alone, the change can serve as a shock. Suddenly, you have to provide your own phone, your own car, your own expenses – your own desk! Beware of making such a move, and ensure that your working relationship with the artist and the artist's record company is both potentially lucrative and legally watertight. Don't ever make such a move without the assistance of a lawyer and an accountant.

THE LONE MANAGER

Having dissuaded those would-be artists from rushing to employ a lone friend or follower as their manager, it has to be said that a large proportion of artists' managers in the music business are one-man-bands, operating from a lonely office or even a bedroom, looking after just one act that they've known for some time. Such set-ups can work, but not without much mutual trust, respect and hard work on the part of both manager and managed.

To reiterate a point made earlier: do bear in mind what's needed to run a business, any business, before you set up on your own. Managing an artist doesn't simply mean ringing up a few pubs for gigs and maybe booking the odd rehearsal studio on someone's behalf. If the artist or artists in question are serious, they will want publishing deals, demo tapes made (which are costly), gigs, publicity and ultimately a record deal, followed by radio airplay and television appearances. When an artist reaches these stages of a career, the money is usually available to pay for cars, hotels, transatlantic phone bills, lawyers' fees, etc. At the start, however, such a cash flow simply doesn't exist and, if you've taken on the task of managing an artist without any financial backing at all, either you or your future star (or stars) are going to become dissatisfied.

Beware, too, the casual management deal. You decided to manage your beloved schoolfriend and, with a handshake, tell him or her that you don't want any money now – 'wait until your famous'. That schoolfriend may be a much-adored and much-trusted person, but fame and money do strange things to people. Where will you be, having spent 5 years of your life supporting this person, only to be dumped, without a contract, when the cash finally does start to flow? Don't do anything without payment, or at least a promise of payment enshrined in a legally binding contract. Consult a lawyer before you take on an artist as manager and get all these details thrashed out at the start. If this friend remains the much-liked and trusted person you always thought he or she was, then you'll get your just rewards when the millions pour in anyway. If the relationship goes wrong, a contract might at least provide your with some compensation for the trauma you suffer as you watch your dedicated artist friend turn into a money-crazed monster!

WHAT DOES A MANAGER DO?

You've heeded all the warnings, and are now in your first day behind the manager's desk. What does the day hold in store for you?

In the music business the manager's job is not always that clear cut. For example, Status Quo's manager Bob Young plays occasional harmonica for the band, on record and on stage, and has co-written many of their hits. Most enjoyable for Mr Young: he gets some of the fun that can be had on stage but only a little of the pressure, earns writer's royalties as well as a manager's fee and doesn't have to suffer the consequences of being too famous a face.

But such a position is rare. Most managers are in the background, sweating buckets over unpaid or late fees and royalty cheques; dealing with lawyers, record companies and PR people; coordinating tour dates with studio time and holidays; pushing for better record company deals; telling the temperamental artist that everything's going to be all right and smiling when the temperamental artist takes his or her temper out on the manager.

Put off? Don't be. To manage properly requires true skill and a strong element of creativity. A manager has to find and negotiate the right record and publishing contracts. In collaboration with the artists, the manager must find the right record producer. When a record is to be released the manager must liaise with and, in some cases, employ the plugger. A manager decides upon and works with the concert promoter, hires a publicist and buys advertising. An artist's record won't succeed without good management, and in that case neither will the artist.

A manager is an employer, of a whole range of service providers including publicity people, lawyers and accountants. A manager is a guide and mentor where the artist is concerned, and a great handler of money where just about everyone is concerned. And a manager's reward, apart from the 15%, 20% or even 25% (a lot of money if you have a world star on your hands), is the knowledge that he or she has played a crucial role in the creation of a star act and a string of hit shows and records, not always a thankless task perhaps.

CHOOSING YOUR ARTIST

This has to be done at whatever level you've reached as a manager and can happen in a number of ways. We've talked about the two schoolfriends equation, the creative one and the level-headed one who are convinced that together they will make a good team. And they might. On the other hand, you are more likely simply to decide that you want to be a manager first, and then take on the task of teaming up with client or clients.

Where do you find them? If you are part of an established company, then they will come to you. And it is here that your judgement can make or break your reputation. Choose an act destined for failure, or at least more than one act that's destined for failure, and your reputation as a manager will fail too. You will want to see gigs, hear songs and generally research an act and its relevance to the current market most thoroughly before you sign on the dotted line. Good instincts and a thorough knowledge of the music scene will be valuable here, and this is a key reason why when starting out as a manager it would be helpful to have gained experience of the industry, and the wider the better, in any way possible.

THE DEAL

Artists should bear in mind that managers are in it for the money. What else? That money usually amounts to around 15–20% of an artist's gross earnings. If the manager doubles as agent (Chapter 16) there will be a further 10% or so on top of that. So the struggling artist could end up saying goodbye to some 35% of his or her earnings. This should only be a cause for concern to the artist should the manager not be doing a reasonable job, in which case the contract should be terminated. Remember, therefore, that both artist and manager should check that such a termination would not be too costly for either party. And this is where your lawyers come in (Chapter 6).

MANAGEMENT: DOING THE JOB

In the case of a new act picked up by a manager, most of the work to be done will be related to the establishment of the act in question. Let's say the act in question is a band with a wide repertoire comprising the members' own compositions; it plays live regularly and is building a large following. The manager taking on this band will want to consider these points:

- The band's intended career path. What is the manager expected to achieve? A publishing deal? Record deal? Live appearances? Where does the band see its future? Does the band seek worldwide success, and if so to what extremes is the manager allowed to go in order to achieve these goals?

- The terms of the deal. What is the manager's percentage, what is the duration of the management contract and what is the extent of that contract? Does it include management of all affairs, and if so will the 80:20 (or whatever) deal include all earnings?

- Does the band want exclusive management? If so, the 80:20 might have to be stretched to, say, 70:30

- A business plan. This will be the manager's next stage, once the band and management have agreed terms. This will, to some extent, be cast in stone and used in situations where, for example, the manager might want to raise a loan from a bank or another investor.

In the day-to-day running of a band, the manager's role can involve anything from talking with record company A&R people about record deals to lunching with publishers and meeting with concert promoters and booking agents. In the case of a band with all deals in place – publishing deal, record deal and a deal with a concert promoter – the manager's job will essentially involve seeing that the terms of all those deals are adhered to by all parties and administering the deals on behalf of the band on a day-to-day basis.

In the case of the record deal with an album in the making the manager will, on a daily basis, want to ensure that:

- the record company's A&R department provides suitable support without interfering with the band's creative input;
- the record company press office or hired-in PR company understands the band and its wishes with regard to publicity;
- the marketing department times its campaign properly with the release of the album and that media advertising and in-store promotions are properly targeted.

In the case of a forthcoming tour which has been taken on by a promoter the manager will, on a daily basis, want to ensure that:

- the tour and album release are properly coordinated to maximize publicity benefits of the tour on the album;
- the right venues are being chosen, and the right conditions offered at the venues by the venue management;
- that the tour contract is being adhered to and that all artists' riders are observed;
- that the tour is being properly promoted at local, national and (if relevant) international level.

In the case of a publishing deal the manager will, on a daily basis, want to ensure that:

- the publisher is properly promoting the catalogue and song-writing skills of the act in question for possible exploitation by other artists (if indeed that's what the writers want);
- there are other publishers who might be waiting in the wings to buy out the publishing of the act.

If manager and/or publisher work to raise the value of the catalogue in question, both will benefit if it sells and manager and artists will benefit if the old publishing deal is renewed at a higher price.

In general, the good manager will always be on the look out

for new and profitable ways of exploiting the talents of his or her act, while at the same time maximizing earnings and properly managing the income from existing work.

GAINING EXPERIENCE

The following chapters in this book will outline key music business jobs and how they relate to each other. All relate to the job of manager, as a manager needs to know what's happening to an artist from the songwriting and rehearsal stage right through to the point at which the money goes into the artist's bank and the record shoots up the charts. If you are uncertain as to whether or not the manager's job is for you, read on to learn exactly what and who you will be dealing with along the route to your artist's success. That will help you to make up your mind.

5

The publisher

To the outsider, the role of the publisher in the modern-day music business is perhaps the most bewildering of all. We all know what a book publisher does: a book publisher pays a writer (in the form of an advance and royalties) to write a book and then finances the printing, marketing and distribution of that book in return for a share in the profits. Music publishing is different. It is the record company that pays for the printing (or, rather, pressing or stamping) and marketing of a record, not the publisher. Likewise, when you buy a record it is the company's name that is emblazoned on the label, not the publisher's. You usually have to look very closely for the publisher's name; you'll eventually find it, in a tiny typeface, squeezed up against the edge of the label so as not to spoil the artwork. What has the publisher done in return for this dubious credit? Before answering that question, it's worth taking a look at the role of the publisher of old, the publisher who, before the mass marketing of recorded music, was credited in a considerably larger typeface.

THE EARLY PUBLISHERS

Before the days of the singer–songwriter and the boom in recorded popular music, publishing *was* the music business. Money was earned mainly by the selling of songs and music by publishers to performers. Publishers would acquire the copyright to a writer's work in return for a small fee. The publisher would then seek to exploit this work by getting it performed on stage, in clubs, on the radio and later on record, through a network of artists' agents and managers. The work might also be exploited by the publishing and retailing of the words and music in sheet form. The publisher would then pay the writer a small proportion of any money earned from his or her song in this way. This sum of money is called a *royalty* payment.

Prolific and/or popular writers during this time might be signed long term to a publisher, receiving a small wage in return for the regular delivery of new works for the publisher to market. It is generally regarded that such arrangements were weighted heavily in the publisher's favour as the contract would effectively render the writer *out of bounds* to anyone else, while at the same time serving to enhance the publisher's reputation as a nurturer of good talent and reliable provider of material.

Many artists were very badly exploited during this era, and before the establishment of *collecting societies* (see below) the mafia-style tactics used by less reputable publishers both to get their songs performed and subsequently to collect their dues did not enhance the reputation of the profession.

ALL CHANGE

The business of music publishing went through a radical change with the arrival of the singer–songwriter who before Buddy Holly in the US and Lennon and McCartney in the UK was very much the exception rather than the rule. Up until the arrival of The Beatles, the popular music charts on both sides of the Atlantic were made up largely of songs from shows and films, or songs recorded by popular music artists, often with a jazz or music hall background. Rarely were the performers of these works credited with writing them as well; these were songs which had been successfully *placed* with artists by publishers, who in turn were earning large sums from them.

In May 1960, for example, the number one album in the US was the soundtrack to the film *The Sound of Music*, while the number one album in the UK was the soundtrack to the film *South Pacific*. In May 1964, the number one album in the US was *The Beatles' Second Album*, while the number one album in the UK was *The Rolling Stones* by The Rolling Stones.

Once The Beatles and others had proved that there was a breed of artist that could provide its own material, the relationship between the publisher and the rest of the industry started to change. With the emergence of the singer–songwriter, there was a shift of power away from the publisher and into the hands of the artist and the record company. After all, if a record company signs an artist or group of artists who have also proved themselves as writers, the record company is unlikely in the future to have any problems finding songs for those artists. So, as first The Beatles and The Rolling Stones in the UK and Bob Dylan and The Beach Boys in the US proved their abilities to come up with hits, time after time, so the record companies began actively seeking artists and groups who could offer similar – performance and songwriting in one single *package*.

As this trend continued, the record companies then began to ask themselves why, as the discoverers and nurturers of all this singing–songwriting talent, they should not be acting as publishers as well. So many of the record companies which hadn't yet done so established their own publishing companies.

In fact, what has happened since is that most artists have still kept their recording and publishing deals separate; few are recorded and published by the same company, as better publishing deals are usually struck if the two remain independent from each other. There are also those artists who publish themselves, thus personally retaining the rights, and hence all the publishing royalties, to all their own work. Not all are happy to do this, however, as to run a publishing company properly requires time, organization and even staff. Properly run, however, music publishing companies can make large sums of money, which is why most large record companies retain publishing operations whether or not their own artists sign to them.

A PUBLISHING DEAL TODAY

Let's take the example of a female singer–songwriter with proven songwriting talent, and hopefully longevity, who has at long last signed a record deal. The artist in question has decided to go for a separate publishing deal which has been negotiated by her manager in the wake of the signing of the record deal.

In exchange for the signing over of the rights to a body of

existing work, everything written by this artist in the past 2 years, plus all subsequent compositions for the next 10 years (some sign for life, others for as little as 2 or 3 years), the publisher has agreed to pay an advance of, say, £10 000. If after 10 years our artist is still at the top of her profession, much sought after and selling hundreds of thousands of records, then the publisher will of course attempt to extend this deal. There will, however, be 101 publishers knocking at her door at that time, all offering more than the next guy can, so a short-term contract could serve as a good investment if an artist's career goes well.

International

The publishing company to which our artist has signed is not an international organization, so it can't exploit the artist's product worldwide within the framework of its own operation, but it does have a network of overseas publishers with whom it can negotiate deals, and this is the route that artist, publisher and manager have decided to take. Another alternative would be for the artist's manager (or lawyer) to negotiate separate deals with overseas publishers on the artist's behalf. The advantage of this would be that her domestic publisher would not be entitled to any forthcoming overseas earnings; the disadvantage, however, would be that the management would not necessarily have the network of contacts available to the domestic publisher and so every separate foreign deal would have to be negotiated from scratch, and this could be both time-consuming and costly.

ROYALTIES

Even today, not all big-name popular music artists are singer–songwriters; most are though, and even those who are not will always be advised at least to have a go at writing the B-side as there is money to be earned this way from mechanical *rights*.

Mechanical rights, or *mechanicals*, is the right to record a piece of music. Anyone who records a copyright piece of music (Chapter 17) needs permission to do so, and this permission will usually be given in return for a royalty which is paid to the owner of the song. In the case of our artist, the owner is the publisher, who receives the payment and then pays the artist her share in accordance with the terms of the publishing contract. If the copyright work is being recorded for use in a film, a commercial or a television show, then the sum payable (known as a *synchronization* fee) is usually negotiated between the publisher and the person using the music. If, on the other hand, the music is being recorded for retail sale, in other words to be sold as a record in a record shop, then there is a set royalty rate as laid down by the Mechanical Copyright Protection Society (MCPS).

The Mechanical Copyright Protection Society

The MCPS represents thousands of composers and publishers of music in the UK and, by reciprocal agreements with sister organizations in other countries, also represents many more the world over. The MCPS licenses those record companies and other organizations and individuals who record its members' copyright works and collects and distributes the royalties payable under those copyrights. MCPS also licenses the importation of recorded music from outside the European Union.

The Performing Rights Society

The other source of income for the songwriter is from *performing rights*, in other words the money paid by organizations which perform or broadcast songs for public consumption. These organizations include radio and television stations, dance halls, pubs, restaurants, hotels and even hospitals. Every time you hear a piece of music in a lift, the chances are that, however unpleasant that music may sound to you, the owner of that lift is paying royalties on it! Radio and television stations log every piece of music they use and pay accordingly, while the other aforementioned establishments will most likely pay a licence fee based on a number of factors, such as how much music is played, for what purpose and to how many people.

In the UK, performing rights payments and licence fees are collected by the Performing Rights Society (PRS) and its affiliated organizations around the world, which in turn pay its many thousands of registered publishers and songwriters. The PRS is effectively an association of publishers and composers, representing over 20 000 members in the UK and a further 500 000 foreign publishers and composers through reciprocal agreements with societies around the world. (The US equivalent of the PRS is the American Society of Composers, Publishers and Authors, ASCAP.) Figures for 1992 had PRS collecting £156m and MCPS £94m.

For publishers with several hundred songwriters on their books, PRS and MCPS income combined is not to be sniffed at, for it is primarily the publishers' job to collect these payments and finally pass them on to their writers, after first taking their cut, of course.

The publisher's cut

Thankfully for today's songwriters, the old 50:50 days are over. Publishers used to take 50% of the royalties earned by their artists. However, the establishment of the singer–songwriter, the competition posed to publishers by the publishing arms of record companies and the rise of the self-publishing writers together mean that today a fairer split is the norm.

An 80:20 or 85:15 split in the artist's favour is more common these days; some top-name artists might even take 100% of their royalties, with the publisher relying on the prestige of that artist to attract others of similar calibre (usually only the publishing arm of a major record company can afford such a luxury). What this change in the royalty split means is that publishers today can no longer afford to act simply as glorified banks, collecting their clients' royalties, earning a bit of interest on the way and then paying out a proportion minus the publisher's cut. To survive today, publishers need to be creative, to make their clients' songs work for them and to invest in back-catalogue which can be re-exploited in new ways. The CD boom of the mid-eighties which ran into the early nineties presented an opportunity for much back-catalogue to be dusted down and re-presented to the public at large. While such an opportunity is unlikely to occur again on such a large scale, publishers who don't actively seek new avenues will lose out to those who see the rights they own as more than just a tap dripping cash.

WHAT A PUBLISHER DOES

What the job of a music publisher entails depends very much on the size of the publishing company, the nature of its signings and what it is the publisher hopes to get out of the business.

Many publishers will specialize, gaining a reputation for looking after a certain type of writer/artist. Others, meanwhile, will simply amass as many *properties* as possible, hoping that most or many of them will simply earn money by themselves. After all, if you own the rights to, say, the musical *West Side Story*, it will go on earning for you for as long as those rights remain in your possession. Little has to be done to encourage people the world over to perform and broadcast that particular collection of songs, although there are those publishers who will strive to make even the most bankable of properties work for them in ways others might never have considered.

For example, Paul McCartney – still one of the world's highest earning rock stars – makes most of his money these days not by writing, recording and selling new records (although he still earns more than acceptable amounts in this way), but by giving live performances of his back-catalogue (some of the rights to which he owns, though not all) and by exploiting other people's work as a publisher. His publishing company owns the rights to the songs of Buddy Holly. It's a very popular back-catalogue, and one which still enjoys good radio airplay the world over, particularly with the rise in popularity of so-called 'gold' radio stations, which play only oldies, mainly from the fifties, sixties and seventies. McCartney and his publishing company have worked to promote the Holly catalogue in a number of ways, notably by arranging an annual Buddy Holly Day to commemorate the late star's birthday, which gives the media good reason to make reference to the star and for radio and television programmes to feature his work, thus serving to keep Holly's name alive. Clearly McCartney is a fan and would maintain that it is Holly's memory that is most important here. Nonetheless, such an event can't fail to maintain the value of the late star's catalogue.

Publishers will always be looking out for new ways in which to promote existing catalogue. The trend for using old rock classics in television advertisements, sparked in the eighties by the Levi's campaign, persists into the nineties and it would be a foolish publisher of back-catalogue that would ignore such a potentially lucrative market.

Publishers will also have one eye on titles whose copyrights have reverted back to the author or to the author's estate, and will be aware of films in the making which will require a soundtrack.

New talent

Much of the role of the publisher described so far involves back-catalogue, and as such might give the impression that this is an industry full of reactionary types who simply live in, and milk, the past. Well, some might say that is a very good description of a section of the music publishing industry. Yet it is certainly not the whole story.

For there are new writers and artists emerging all the time, almost all of whom will spend a fair proportion of their lives struggling to make a living from their work. As with the A&R departments (Chapter 7), it is these people the publishers ignore at their peril. Back-catalogue may be lucrative, but it needed to be created from scratch in the first place by people who were once new to this business with no track record. The toughest job for anyone in the music business is to spot new talent, to have faith in that talent – faith that will allow you to commit both time and financial resources to that talent. A proactive publisher will succeed here by keeping in touch with A&R departments and the live scene.

Publishers with the ability and initiative to discover new, unsigned talent (some publishing companies will have their own A&R equivalents working as full-time talent scouts) are in a good position whenever such an act signs with a record company and begins to make and sell records. In such a case, a forward-thinking publisher would finance a *demo* tape (a professional-standard recording which *demonstrates*, hence demo, the quality of the act and its songs) which the act can use to get live work and, with any luck, an audience with a record company A&R person. If a record deal does arise from such proactive work from a publisher, the publisher might attempt to negotiate *points*, or a percentage of earnings, from the record deal. Artists' managers, who will usually be the people to negotiate the record deal, will try to avoid this, however, as this can complicate a contract. The publisher will, after all, be earning royalties from the publishing deal, and these will increase the more success the act enjoys under the record deal.

Some publishers in the position described above will take on the additional role of manager themselves.

Administration

As well as the creative, exciting elements of the job of the music publisher, there is also much routine administration involved. Contracts have to be drawn up, for which lawyers are required (Chapter 6); collecting societies have to be dealt with; record companies have to be badgered (are they promoting the artist properly?); writers too; an office has to be run; taxes and staff have to be paid; and books have to balance.

If you're a singer–songwriter who has set up your own publishing operation simply to look after your own compositions, the administrative responsibilities can be relatively minimal. You will have joined PRS and MCPS (and these societies will pay the affiliated author's dues whether or not he or she actually forms a publishing company), and will probably pay a lawyer and accountant for occasional services which will include the administration of these royalties.

Generally, however, publishers can do as little or as much as they like with regards to *working their catalogue*. If they do just a little, they will get away with it as long as the artists/catalogues concerned have a life of their own. If, on the other hand, they take a hands-on approach to the work they publish, there is much pleasure and much money to be had from the business.

PUBLISHING: DOING THE JOB

Throughout this chapter, the term *the publisher* has been used to refer to the publishing company rather than the person. There are few one-man or one-woman publishing outfits; large concerns might employ 50 and even 100 people, while smaller independents might survive on a managing director and a handful of administrative staff.

The typical day for the managing director (MD) of a small independent publishing concern might be as follows:

- First thing: open mail, much of which will be routine letters from lawyers, record companies, songwriters or managers of songwriters already signed to the company and, of course, bills. A proportion of the day's mail will comprise demo tapes from hopeful writers. These should be listened to as soon as possible and returned if the MD is not interested. There will also be those tapes which warrant a second listen. If it is decided that one or more of these is worth further investigation the MD might set this in motion.

- Routine business: there will be ongoing tasks which will be dealt with after the daily routines are taken care of. These could be anything from drawing up new publishing deals to renewing old ones. There will be staff who warrant the MD's attention. If there is a talent scout employed in the company he or she might well have been out the night before checking on a couple of live acts and, if so, will want to discuss them with the MD.

- Lunch: usually lunch offers the opportunity for the MD to maintain or develop relationships with existing or potential clients. Lunch might therefore be at a restaurant with one of the writers signed to the company or the writer's manager, or possibly with the manager of a writer the MD is hoping to sign.

- After lunch: there will be calls to return, possibly more tapes to listen to and the afternoon might be a good time to pitch songs. A publisher signs up a writer either because that writer has an outlet for those songs as a performer or band member, or because the writer's songs are so strong that eventually, it is hoped, those songs will be performed and recorded by high-earning artists. Pitching your writers' songs can be done in a number of ways, but it is almost always done through a network of contacts the publisher and staff has built up over the years. So, when pitching a writer's songs, the publisher will want them to be heard by anyone who is anyone in the music: artists' managers, A&R people (a notoriously difficult route), record producers and even the artists themselves if the publisher has good relationships with any of them.

- The afternoon over, most people are keen to get home and do anything but work. However, as with most areas of the music business, the evening is a time when the publisher is likely to come across new writers, singing and playing their songs in clubs and pubs. Few proactive MDs will let such opportunities go by unless the company in question is so big that there are talented and trusted talent scouts paid to do this on the MD's behalf.

GETTING INTO PUBLISHING

To know where, how and when a piece of music can be exploited, and to what extent is critical to the success of a music publishing operation. Such skills are best learned within a music publishing company, although most such organizations pay all but top-level staff small amounts for their efforts. It is important to note that, taking the music industry as a whole, publishing is a small employer (some 2000 people in all are employed in this area of the business) and the work is specialized; these two factors combined mean that getting in will be tough and you will not earn fortunes unless you climb high.

To join the publishing arm of one of the multinational record companies such as EMI or Sony might serve as a more solid background to the music publishing business, and depending on what level you wish to join at this could be done with certain qualifications and minimal experience.

Legal qualifications would always help here, along with a demonstrable understanding of copyright. General legal qualifications (rather than specifically musical or showbusiness) can be acquired in a number of ways, and such qualifications coupled with a broad knowledge of music and an understanding of the industry will also help.

In music publishing it is generally regarded that around 75% of the jobs are administrative positions, the remainder being on the *creative* side. Administrative jobs include royalty manager (overseeing the flow of royalties into the company and seeing that they are properly administered); financial controller; business affairs manager (making certain that creative decisions make business sense – effectively playing a significant role in the overall running of the company); and several junior administrative posts below these.

It is these administrative jobs, in which a clear head, numeracy, literacy and reliability are all important, that are the easiest to get as a beginner. Keep an eye on the music trade papers for advertisements and also write to publishing companies on a regular basis (details of music publishing bodies appear at the back of this book). As we have said before, music publishing in the UK employs only 2000 people (not including the songwriters) so the *ins* are few and far between.

The so-called *creative* jobs are small in number and usually sit at the top of the company. The managing director (see above), the creative director (who would make decisions about the creative direction of the company and broad policy decisions about signings and management of catalogue) and the A&R manager (if there is one) will most likely be recruited from within the business: any publisher will tell you that, at the top, it's who you know as much as what you know.

Your ultimate aim might be to run your own publishing company. If this is the case, you should consider the low-paid work you get to begin with as an investment in the future. Learn as much as you can as an employee and then take off and gain general business qualifications. In just a few years time you could be the person sitting with your feet up on your desk puffing away at a cigar. Or, better still, you could be the person who kills that hackneyed image of the publisher once and for all!

6

The negotiators

There have been 101 books written about rock and roll rip-offs. When you think of the enormity of some of them – just how much of an artist's hard-earned cash was being siphoned off by managers and others in so many of these cases – you start to wonder what it is about rock stars, rock managers or the rock business that allows this to happen so frequently.

To go into the minute detail of actual cases here would take several books (and those books do exist!), but suffice it to say that the biggest names of the last 30 years, from The Beatles to Elton John, from The Rolling Stones to Sting, have all been ripped off in some way and have spent a large proportion of their lives in court trying to rectify their situations. Why don't they learn from past cases? Why do management, publishing and recording contracts repeatedly have to be dismantled in court in order for the artists to get their just deserts? Why can't the business be simplified so that artists simply do what's required of them and get paid accordingly?

Here's the short answer to all these questions: in music, you're dealing with a product with *no intrinsic value*. It is nonetheless a product from which there is *much money* to be made. To get from *no intrinsic value* to *much money* involves the manipulation and exploitation of a whole range of people and businesses, which is done through a series of contracts drawn up between artist and publisher, artist and manager, artist and record company. To get from *no intrinsic value* to *much money* also requires an understanding of the marketplace – who buys records, when and why? To get from *no intrinsic value* to *much money* also requires an understanding of the concept of royalties – whose cut is whose, at what stage is the cut taken and when?

Most important in all this, of course, is the creator of the music. Without him, her or them, the business doesn't exist. But a creator of music usually starts out young without having acquired any experience of the above, has no interest in the above and is so busy writing and playing, in the early days at least, that he, she or they have no time to deal with the business side.

Hence the rip-offs. Struggling artists who believe 100% in their creations but who are not making any money from them are perfect targets for shrewd wheeler-dealers. How many artists are going to ignore the person who shows an interest in their work, who believes in what they're doing and who offers the opportunity to make money from it?

ARE THEY ALL OUT TO GET YOU?

In the US, you are advised to get a lawyer even before you learn how to play an instrument! Things haven't got quite that bad in the UK yet, and it is important at this point to put the idea of the rock and roll rip-off into some kind of perspective. Not everyone wants to rip off their artists, and often many so-called rip-offs are no more than badly negotiated contracts.

As was explained in Chapter 4, in the early days of an artist's career, an 85:15 management contract might not seem too outrageous. After all, if he or she got you the £25 gig, £3.75 is a fairly reasonable fee to offer in return. But what did your initial contract with that manager say about future earnings? And what did it say about earnings in which the manager plays no part?

Many of the large-scale superstar court cases have been about getting out of age-old contracts which have no relevance to the present day; contracts which see people who now have little to do with your career still earning from your efforts.

That is not to say that the master of the rip-off doesn't exist. Rip-offs happen in all businesses, masterminded by people who see such behaviour as simply another way of making money. And that is why so many get away with it; because they themselves believe that what they're doing is fair game, they are able to carry out their dirty deeds in a convincing, 'everything's fine and above-board' manner.

BRINGING IN THE NEGOTIATORS

An artist's first contract is most likely to be with a manager. It may be with a booking agent (Chapters 13 and 19) if, in the early days, the artist or artists are running their own affairs, but it's unlikely that things will work that way around. The first few gigs will most likely be small ones which will not involve an agent. Once the act in question goes up a few rungs on the live circuit, a manager is most likely to have been brought in and he or she will then be signing contracts with agents and venues.

So, it's the management contract which will be the first to receive the artist's signature (hopefully a signature that will one day be collectable!) and it is at this point that the lawyer is brought in.

This might sound a rather expensive and somewhat dramatic move, but if the manager has had a proper contract drawn up, something that says more than simply 'I get 20% of everything' (and that won't be sufficient), then it will require a lawyer to check it through in detail, on the artist's behalf.

The right manager

The artist is advised not to take on the first manager that shows an interest (Chapter 4). The artist is also advised not to go for a friend as a manager, except in exceptional circumstances. The manager the artist chooses should have an interest in and a knowledge of the music business which exists independently of the act. After all, if the would-be manager's interest is simply a passion for this particular act and doesn't go beyond that, well, there's a danger of that passion waning and then where does that leave the artist?

Word of mouth works best here. Artists should talk to other like-minded acts and seek recommendations from them. The would-be manager should understand the artists and their goals, should at least understand – if not like – the music, where it sits in the marketplace as a whole, and how and in which direction it might progress.

The right lawyer

Having found the right manager, the artist will then need to sign the management contract. This is where all the problems can begin, so this should only be done once the artist is independently represented by a lawyer. The lawyer will study the contract in detail, and ask for some clauses to be removed and others to be added, until such time as he or she is happy that the artist has a good deal – and one that will remain good for the duration of the contract in accordance with the way in which it is presumed the artist's career will progress.

It should not be any old lawyer, however. A music business lawyer is required, and the artist finds him or her by word of mouth or on advice from a body that exists to serve the interest of artists, such as the Musicians' Union. The lawyer will understand the workings of the industry, will hopefully have some knowledge of the artist's prospective manager and will again bear in mind the likely path the artist's career will take before giving the artist the final go-ahead to sign.

The lawyer will cost money. Many will carry out such a service at a relatively low cost on the understanding that the artist will request his or her services again in the future – hopefully when the stakes are higher and the lawyer can charge considerably more.

Artists who avoid paying a lawyer at this early stage do so at their peril. They might have to scrimp and save to pay this first lawyer's bill but it will be worth it, for a badly worded contract could cost the artist dearly in later life, and that small saving will be regretted forever.

ONCE THE MANAGER'S ON BOARD

There is a school of thought that says that once you have the right manager you will never have to worry about another contract again. And in most cases this will be true. Once the manager has become part of the team, it is for the artists to make and perform the music, and for the manager to manage the business of exploiting both the artists and the artists' product for commercial gain. If the manager's contract with the artist is watertight, and effectively only allows the manager to earn if the artist does, then the manager will from here onwards work to maximize the artist's profits.

Suffice it to say, however, that a manager too can make mistakes – a manager can also be tempted to strike deals with record companies, concert promoters and merchandising companies which work in the manager's favour but to the detriment of the artist. Independent legal advice will therefore always be required by the artist whenever a contract is negotiated by the management on the artist's behalf.

IS A MANAGER NEEDED?

In the US it is common for lawyers to do much of the manager's work. There are many American artists who have built successful careers without ever having signed a management deal, and this way of doing business has caught on in the UK in recent years.

The benefits of working in this way are obvious. Lawyers in the UK are barred from taking percentages from the artists employed by them, and so lawyer's flat fees replace the manager's negotiated percentage. Also, a lawyer will be working for the artist and only the artist. Unlike the manager, whose relationship with the record company might be important for reasons unrelated to a deal with a specific artist (good long-term relationships with record companies will always be beneficial to a manager or management company), a lawyer dealing with the record company on the artist's behalf will not be concerned about his or her relationship with the record company and so will be free to act as ruthlessly as negotiations might require.

If an artist does decide to use lawyers, or a series of lawyers, to strike the various deals required during the course of his or her career and to do without the services of a manager, that artist will have to have a very clear idea of where his or her career is going, for a manager does other things besides signing deals. A manager can be crucial to the development of an artist's career in terms of steering the artist in the right direction, looking for and finding new areas for the artist to exploit, such as film, television, product endorsement and merchandising, and is generally around to serve as a troubleshooter in any and every area if and when required. Managers often prove most useful when it comes to looking after money and even deciding what to do with any excess.

THE MONEY: ACCOUNTANTS AND FINANCIAL ADVISERS

Artists who are new to the business will often be tempted to start spending like crazy as soon as the money starts rolling in. After years of struggle and poverty such a reaction is natural. Yet this is always inadvisable. As already described, an advance is almost always paid against future royalties and in the early days should be used carefully not only to provide wages for the artists, but also to buy equipment, pay for rehearsal time and generally to invest in the artist's or artists' future.

Careful administration and negotiation of advances can help to reduce the artist's tax liabilities. There are many other less obvious ways of making the money work for an artist which only a good accountant with solid music business experience will know about.

So here is another negotiator whose value must be weighed up against the possible cost. An accountant or experienced financial adviser will be able to find creative ways in which a large advance or a large lump sum royalty payment might be used instead of it simply being distributed equally among musicians, managers and writers. We hear of rock stars owning houses and apartments the world over. Why? They can only live in one at a time, but do they also serve to reduce an artist's tax bill?

And why are the tax bills of rock and roll's wealthiest constantly in the news? Surely, if they're making that much money not only can they afford to pay big tax bills but they ought to be obliged to pay them. There is a great deal of truth in this. The problem with the rock and roll business is that often the bulk of a successful artist's riches is earned over a comparatively short period of time, say 2 or 3 years, yet will often have to serve to pay for previous fallow years and any low-earning years which may come later. An artist who earns a million pounds in 1 year risks being taxed as someone who earns a million pounds every year, even if he or she genuinely earns nothing the next. At the time an artist faces such a situation, the creative accountant or financial adviser suddenly becomes the most important person on the team!

LOSING TOUCH

Just how much control an artist and or manager can have over the artist's product is hard to measure. How can an artist know how many tickets a concert promoter sold at any one gig? If the hall was clearly full to capacity, and the hall took 1000 people, then 1000 tickets' worth of takings would be expected. But then there is the *'rubber walls syndrome'*, whereby the promoter allows more than the fire-regulated 1000 people into the venue and pockets the difference. How can the artist and/or manager always be aware of such a fiddle? And how can an artist and/or manager know how many of a record company's declared *unsold* records were genuinely unsold? How can an artist know how many copies of a record have sold in Peru or Sri Lanka?

There are several agencies and organizations which exist to protect musicians' and composers' earnings, but none can claim a 100% success rate. Even the well-established PRS and MCPS systems are open to abuse (Chapters 5 and 17). At some point the artist and all the negotiators employed to carry out various tasks at various times have to decide that the double-checking and the surveillance should stop. Otherwise, the music business starts to look less like a source of entertainment and more like an international spy ring in which everyone is under suspicion and considered guilty until proven innocent.

7

The A&R person

One still hears people in the business referring to the A&R *man*. This is partly because the term rolls nicely off the tongue. Some maintain that the term *man* in this case is an abbreviation of the word *manager*. But also, in the past, A&R was regarded as a rather tough job, only for those who were prepared to dedicate themselves 100% to the record company and to the music. No social life, no regular office hours. In the male-dominated record business of the sixties and seventies it was therefore considered that women would neither stand for this nor be able to take the pressure. However, the eighties and nineties have seen an increasing number of A&R women succeed in the industry so today the blanket term A&R man is not just sexist but also inaccurate.

Record companies are in business to sell recorded music, and that music has to come from somewhere. A&R is the department within a record company which finds that music, its writers and performers and then decides whether or not the company should invest in them.

To carry out this work, an A&R person needs to be constantly networking – getting out there, meeting people, finding out what and who is in, what and who is out, which record companies are in search of what type of act and why. This is extraordinarily tough work. It involves going out most nights of most weeks to see and hear people playing in smoky clubs and pubs the length and breadth of the country and often further afield. It involves being cornered by managers, who might not be the type of people you would want to spend an evening with, and staying up late after the gig with an act which is desperate for you not to leave until at least a couple of encouraging words have passed your lips.

To succeed as an A&R person you've got to love the business, you need to have total dedication to the type of music you're searching for and you must grow a very thick skin – to protect you from all the hype, the bribes and anything else which might be thrown at you in a typical week. And, what's more, if you're in a relationship and you want it to last, your partner will have to love the business as much as, if not more than, you!

Back at the office there's more pressure. The record company wants the best talent and a quick return from it. Where's it coming from? Why haven't you found it yet? And why has that band you found that we signed last year not had a hit yet?

The job's not all bad, of course. It can pay very well. Also, if you're totally dedicated to the search for the next great Irish rock band, the next great male middle-of-the-road balladeer or the next great female soul star, see all the above as simply a means to a most satisfying end and, most important, you're 100% confident in your judgement, then A&R is for you.

A&R: THE JOB

Much of the A&R person's time is spent sifting through tapes and letters, taking calls from bands, writers and managers and saying 'no' to most of them. Listening through tape after tape can be a soul-destroying pastime, and most experienced A&R people have acquired a skill which means they don't ever have to listen to more than the first minute of any unsolicited tape. (This may come as heartbreaking news to anyone who has spent hundreds and even thousands of pounds putting together a five-track demo tape simply to send out to A&R departments. On the other hand, such people would, or should, always put their best track first. If the A&R person does like the sound of the first minute, he or she will listen on. More on demo tapes in Chapter 16.)

Experienced A&R people will know that, after the *1-minute listen*, it is important to rewind the tapes back to the start if they intend to return them to the artists concerned (many don't), otherwise the artists would instantly be able to see that only a minute or so of the tape had been played. This would not do a great deal for the artist's confidence.

Both prospective artists and prospective A&R people should note here that A&R departments, generally, do not enjoy turning people down. Their job, after all, is to sign new acts. If they don't, they've failed. So it's important that prospective artists don't see a rejection as a sign of their failure, and also that A&R people don't rush into a signing simply to prove themselves. A&R is tough. Productivity depends upon what's out there; you can't sign your way out of a seemingly dead period, and neither can you sign an act simply to make it or others happy. This sounds like rather an obvious point to make, but all A&R people are at some time during their career faced with the situation that they would love to sign up a particular act, simply because they like the people and want to do them a favour. This is no basis for a signing, however, and all good A&R people will be able to recognize such a temptation and resist it.

Contacts

Unsolicited letters, tapes and calls from hopeful artists will never provide the main source of talent from which an A&R person draws. Good contacts in the business are crucial tools in the search for new talent. A&R people usually build a wide network of contacts including artists' managers, concert promoters, booking agents, producers, pluggers, DJs and retailers, all of whom will have an idea of what's happening in their fields and genres. This network will serve not only to draw the A&R department's attention to new hopefuls, but also to give an idea of who else is taking these new hopefuls seriously. Good A&R people will be proactive rather than reactive in their quest for new talent, but will ignore at their peril the views and opinions of others in the business who are constantly exposed to new, hopeful talent.

Once a new act has caught the eye and the ear of the A&R person, that act will never (or at least very rarely) be signed on the spot, as sometimes happens in the movies. If the A&R person has heard the act by recommendation or by chance, say at a club or in a pub, he or she will next want to meet the person who booked the act, and anyone else who can answer the following questions:

- Has the act got a manager?

- Who writes the material?

- If it's a band, how permanent is the line-up?

- Are any other record companies showing interest (this always gives added incentive to the competitive A&R person)?

- Is the act actually looking for a deal?

- Is there any recorded material to be heard?

- How long has the act been performing this particular set?

The idea here is to build up a practical picture of how this act might work professionally. If the instant gut feeling is 'Wow, this lot are great!', the A&R person should then take a long, calculated look at the act concerned in the cold light of day, simply to ensure that this was more than just the feel-good factor that many live acts are capable of generating on the night, but which won't necessarily translate into good, solid record company product.

Studio-only acts

Most acts are signed on the strength of a live performance and subsequent demo recordings, but there are others who do not play live, or who do so very rarely, who would nonetheless serve a record company well as recording artists. Such acts would most definitely come to the attention of the A&R department via the aforementioned network of contacts, and will often come from another area of the music business.

The Pet Shop Boys, big stars on both sides of the Atlantic during the second half of the eighties and into the nineties, are a classic example of such an act. Both Neil Tennant and Chris Lowe had played in bands before they met but were pursuing musical careers only half-heartedly, in other words they were not out-and-out rock and rollers prepared to live month-in, month-out in sweaty transit vans for the sake of getting up on stage and playing.

After a stint with a folk band, Neil Tennant studied for a degree in history and later became a music journalist, reaching the dizzy heights of deputy editor with the UK's highest circulation pop magazine of the eighties, *Smash Hits*. Lowe, meanwhile, whose father was a musician, had also played in bands, but was studying architecture at the time he met Tennant. The two met in a hi-fi store in 1981, struck up a friendship and started to write and record together. In 1983, while on an assignment in New York interviewing Sting for *Smash Hits*, Tennant got the opportunity to meet his long-time hero, disco producer Bobby 'O' Orlando. After hearing Tennant and Lowe's tapes, Orlando offered to produce the duo. Their first record, West End Girls, was released in a handful of European countries, became a cult hit in a couple of them and then died.

The pair later signed with flamboyant rock manager Tom Watkins (who later became manager of rags-to-riches-to-rags act Bros and others), and a hype built up around the Boys which eventually had A&R people fighting to sign them. EMI won the fight, and nobody needs reminding of the success story which followed.

Now any A&R person active at the time who was not a part of that fight to get The Pet Shop Boys would have been regarded as off the boil unless, of course, The Pet Shop Boys didn't suit the profile of the company in question. The A&R network in that case would have included Watkins in some way, and possibly even Orlando. And Neil Tennant's profile would have been high in the music business anyway because of his *Smash Hits* connections. So you can see how *networking* and generally having a finger on the pulse is absolutely crucial to the business of A&R.

The signing

Once the A&R department is certain it wants to sign a particular act, it is then time to persuade the act in question that this is the company that will serve it best. In most cases, an unsigned act will need little persuasion (and this is the reason why so many get ripped off; Chapter 6), but sometimes, as in the case of The Pet Shop Boys, for example, where there are several companies eager to sign the same act, some serious bargaining will be required.

Few A&R people will be able to negotiate the deal alone; consultation with the company's president, financial director and head of business affairs (if one exists – a lawyer or an accountant might replace either or both of the last two professionals mentioned) will have to take place before a deal is finalized with the band's management. And the perfect deal will have ensured the following: that the signed act respects and trusts the company; that the signed act has sufficient resources to carry out recording and related promotional work; that the company has signed up a strong and long-lasting talent which won't expose it to unnecessary risk; and that the deal will lead to the release of popular product, profitable to both the act in question and the record company. Too good to be true maybe, but these are, or at least should be, the aims of every record deal.

The contract

All contracts are different, although in essence what a recording contract states is how much money will be paid to the various parties involved and for how many albums. Once signed, disputes over contracts can arise as a result of all manner of misinterpretations. Most disputes, however, arise if a band delivers less than was agreed to in the contract or a record company spends less money/time/effort on the act than was promised.

There are two broad types of contract: the recording deal and the *fund* deal. The recording deal usually allows the artist a lump sum on signing and a lump sum on completion and acceptance of the recording, with the record company paying for and administering recording costs in between. In a fund deal, the artist will receive a lump sum at the start to cover both the advance and the recording costs, which the artist and/or artist's manager will administer. This type of deal is usually reserved for big names who switch from one label to another (or who re-sign with their current label), members of big-name bands who re-sign as solo artists, or for those acts over which there has been much fighting between record companies. It is the fund deals, incidentally, which usually spark the *multimillion dollar signing* headlines which occasionally make the papers and which perpetuate the myth that all rock and pop musicians are loaded with money. This is, of course, not the case.

In almost all cases, the contract will be between the record company and the artist or artists. (The contract will usually principally concern the recording of the artist's performance and subsequent sales of those recordings and not the copyright of the recorded songs. Contracts with a publisher would determine ownership of the copyright on a composition; Chapter 5.) A manager will usually negotiate on behalf of the artist, while the draft contract will be discussed and amended by A&R and other record company departments before the final version is agreed upon by legal representatives of both record company and artist's management.

Recording

The A&R department's work is far from finished once the signing has taken place, for it is now that the department has to prove that the right act was signed. A successful recording career now has to be planned, and it is at this point, having found the artist, that the A&R person has to start work on the repertoire.

The artist or artists concerned might find the next few weeks and even months somewhat frustrating. For having been signed on the strength of their performance and their material (if they are writers too), they will presume that they will now be able to go straight into the studio. Well, this is not usually what happens. The repertoire now has to be refined by the A&R person in collaboration with management and artists, and by the producer at some point. Bad material must be thrown out, new material better suited to the studio must be written, and if the artist or artists in question are not writers then material has to be found.

The A&R person must then ensure that the artists know pretty well what's to be recorded and how before studio time is booked. Again in collaboration with management and artist, a producer will then be chosen and hired for the recording session. The job of the producer will then be to combine material and artistic talent to make a record that people will want to buy (Chapter 8). The producer will most likely simply sign a contract for just one album, although some do sign up for a series.

Of course, the more business-like and professional the artist and management, the less worry all of the above will be for the A&R person. It may well be that artist and management make all the recording arrangements and are trusted to do so. If it goes wrong at any point, however, it is the A&R person, as overseer of the whole process, who will take the rap.

Release, marketing and publicity

With recording under way and hopefully on schedule, the A&R person will now keep one eye on the studio (and what it is costing) and the other on release schedules, tour dates and marketing and promotion campaigns. A&R will liaise with all the departments working on aspects of the support of the release, and will be the troubleshooter if any delays occur – perhaps where artwork, TV appearances, tour dates or maybe recording schedules are concerned – and will see to it that all departments realign their efforts accordingly. It is at this stage that the work of the A&R department most overlaps with that of other departments.

THE INDIES AS A&R DEPARTMENTS

The independent labels are often described as self-supporting A&R departments for the majors. Linked to this is a criticism regularly levelled at the majors: that they bother less and less with A&R and, instead, sit around and wait to see what the indies have got to offer and then simply cream off the best.

If a major has its eye on an act signed to an indie, it will usually deal with this in one of the following three ways: it can buy the band, contract and all, while the act is still with the indie; it can wait until the contract between the act in question and the indie is up for renewal; or it can buy the indie itself, as PolyGram did with Island Records, and which effectively meant that PolyGram had bought mega-band U2.

STILL WANT TO BE IN A&R?

As you will have gathered from the above job description, A&R is tough because you're dealing with three basic unknowns, and they are:

- whether or not the act you thought was any good actually is any good;

- whether or not the potential audience really does exist;

- whether or not the people you have signed – including their management – will work and continue to work professionally with you. After all, they are not business people and need not necessarily be qualified in anything in particular. You have signed them for that immeasurable commodity called talent and this, as we all know, is a fragile thing.

So, as an A&R person, you will be like the person at the front of a line of people trying to walk through a forest at night. Nobody knows what's ahead or under foot. What they all do know, though, is that they're all determined to reach their destination in safety and that you are the one who is holding the torch. That's how big an A&R person's responsibility is. If you do make it through the forest, the feeling is truly wonderful and everyone in the line will love you forever, but the journey may not be all fun.

The A&R person's role is nonetheless a crucial one – one which touches upon almost every aspect of the running of a record company. And it is for this reason that so many successful A&R people end up at the top, as managing director and even president of a record company. The going is tough, but the rewards can be considerable. Are you up to it?

HOW TO GET A JOB IN A&R

Retail is not a bad route into A&R. In record retail you will learn about all musical genres, how they fare relative to each other in the marketplace, and what sells when and to whom. Retail will also give you a good idea of how promotion and marketing campaigns work.

Experience with a record company strike force could also provide a good basis for work in A&R. A marketing qualification on top of this would help, plus, of course, demonstration of a continued passion for and understanding of music, artists and the music business generally.

Demonstration of a true desire to get on in the industry is essential, too, if you are ever going to be considered as potential A&R material. It is important not to be too choosy about your first job in the business. If you are good, energetic and can demonstrate that you have an instinctive grasp of what sells and that you are willing and able to work long and unsocial hours, in any area of the music business, this will help you in your quest to become an A&R person.

8

The producer

Brian Eno has described the producer as one of music's 'back-room boys'. Having been on both sides of the glass during the course of his long and illustrious career, as both performer and multiple-award-winning producer in all musical genres, he is as well placed as anyone to define the role. By and large, Eno's description is an accurate one. Most producers do take a back seat when it comes to the fame and notoriety which go hand in hand with success in the music business

Star producers do exist, however; during the dance boom of recent years the role of producer and performer has become blurred, with producers putting together pieces of mainly computerized music, released primarily for club consumption under a whole range of different faceless pseudonyms.

There are also those producers who become star names simply because their role in the creation of a particular sound is impossible to ignore. Trevor Horn is one such producer. Many maintain that eighties' phenomenon ABC and later Frankie Goes To Hollywood would not have had the success they enjoyed without Horn's monster productions. Similarly, US star Meat Loaf has had his best successes when teamed with writer–producer Jim Steinman.

That said, the role of producer is generally well defined within the industry and has been since the late forties and early fifties, during which time the newly introduced magnetic tape (which became available in volume in 1947) was serving as the catalyst which changed the music business from a side show into an international multimillion dollar industry.

THE FIRST PRODUCERS

Before, and in the early days of, magnetic tape, the producer's role was a relatively minor one. The earliest records were recorded directly on to wax, which meant that all mixing and sound balancing such as it was had to be done before the performance to be recorded was given. This meant that the studio engineer's role was considerably more important than that of the producer (if indeed there was one). The studio engineer would have to agree with the performers on the part each voice and instrument was to play, how loud each would be and where each would be positioned for best effect.

Meanwhile, the record company A&R person (which then stood for 'artists and recording', not 'artists and repertoire' as it does today; Chapter 7) would have matched artist with musicians and material, coordinated studio time and so on – all jobs done to a greater or lesser extent these days by the producer, sometimes in collaboration with the fixer (Chapter 18). The producer in the pre-magnetic and early magnetic tape days would arrange the pieces of music prior to recording (if the artists concerned didn't do that themselves) and perhaps conduct the final recorded performance. And that was it.

Today the story is quite different. It was George Martin who, more than any other single person, gave credibility to the idea that a band could retain their world star status even without playing live. Working out new techniques as they went, Martin and The Beatles set standards in studio recording, in terms of technique and innovation, which artists and producers still aspire to today. The Beatles' achievements were not based purely on musical or technical ability; as important to their recordings was a creative urge and a desire to experiment, which, to The Beatles' good fortune, was interpreted to great effect and with great style and affection by George Martin. The Beatles would say 'we want it to sound like this' and Martin, in turn, would know what they meant, find a means of achieving it, often by breaking every rule in the engineer's book, and occasionally take their ideas several steps further, which a producer can only ever do if he or she has the trust and respect of the artists concerned.

Thus the George Martin–Beatles relationship is, to this day, used to illustrate the ideal teaming of artists and producer. Such a relationship has, for many reasons, rarely been replicated since, not least because few bands would be able to afford a producer who was always on call to cater to their every whim, and particularly one who was employed by a record company which also just happened to own one of the world's best recording studios, Abbey Road.

These days the artist–producer relationship is, generally, defined less by a two-way, free flow of creative ideas and more by prevailing fashions and money. These two are often inextricably linked. A band with a track record and a bit of cash behind them will, for their *next* and *long-awaited* album, always be able to put some of their resources towards the buying of the right producer – subject to availability. This will often be a producer whose product is in vogue at that moment and who will therefore lend credibility to the recording.

New artists or bands, on the other hand, will often opt to produce themselves, concerned that an *outsider* producer will either have the effect of stamping the wrong brand name on their music or simply won't understand their needs.

THE PRODUCER'S JOB

The role of the producer in the nineties is infinitely varied. What one can say is that the EMI-employed producer that The Beatles first met at Abbey Road back in June 1962, surrounded and served by engineers in white coats, no longer exists. Producers today are rarely employed permanently by record companies. Rather, they have their favourite artists, record companies, engineers and recording studios, and get work by word of mouth through one or all of these.

A producer in demand will employ a manager or agent, much of whose time is spent saying 'no' or 'you couldn't afford him/her' to hopeful artists and chasing prestige jobs with the top-selling performers or those whom the producer particularly admires.

Back to Brian Eno for a moment. When U2 first approached him to produce their multimillion-selling album *The Joshua Tree*, he turned them down several times. It wasn't so much that he didn't like U2, and it certainly wasn't that they couldn't afford him, or he them; it was simply that he felt that the band would not like what he might do to their music. Eno explained to Bono that it was unlikely that a Brian Eno-produced U2 album would sound like any other U2 album. That, said Bono, was why they wanted him.

Eno's job on that album, and on subsequent U2 recordings, was to listen to the new material that the band had written and, in collaboration with the band, to interpret it for subsequent recording. No two producers work in the same way, and certainly few work in the way Eno does. Much of the truly creative production work that he does with bands takes place while they're not in the studio. He might take a particular sound which the band hadn't thought was particularly significant and, in their absence, bring it out to become a key element of the song in question. Alternatively, he might dismiss almost everything the band did on it. This would provide the basis on which to rebuild the song in an entirely different way.

Many producers play on the records they produce. Some, often to the dismay of the artists concerned, will remove a guitar or keyboard part which had been played by a member of the band and rerecord it themselves.

Here we come to one aspect of the producer's job which can never be taught, at least not formally, and that is diplomacy. The studio is not always a pleasant environment, and the job of recording, as solo artist or as a band, can be fraught with difficulties. A guitarist may feel that a particular song warrants a longer, louder solo; a singer might want fewer or more harmonies; one or all of the performers involved might be feeling down, moody, sick, hung-over, disinterested, resentful, jealous or a combination of some or all of these. It is ultimately down to the producer to respond to this, by gently talking things over with the people concerned, serving as mediator when two artists won't see eye to eye and, in extreme cases, making the decision to postpone the session if things are going particularly badly. Such a decision will always affect budgets and deadlines, however, and so won't be taken lightly.

There are those who regard the producer's job as 80% diplomacy and 20% everything else. For the aspiring producer, it is this diplomacy/studio politics which is the most difficult thing to learn or teach.

So a picture builds of the producer as the person who provides all that is required to make a recording work, which the artists can't or don't provide during either the writing or the recording process. At least, a producer is a musical and logistical arranger and at most he or she is, albeit temporarily, a member of the band whose creative input is as great and often greater than that of any other single member, and sometimes greater than that of the band as a whole.

THE LOGISTICS

The producer is often the person who as well as crafting songs and performances for recording, also finds the session musicians, books the studio, organizes any extra musical or recording equipment that is required, engineers the recording session and controls the recording budget. In many cases, much of this work is carried out by others; producers can rely on tried-and-tested engineers to sort out studios and equipment, on managers or record company people to look after the money (often the A&R manager) and the artist or artists to bring in any extra musicians required. It all depends on the producer, the money that's available, the experience of the artists and how well the producer knows them, the engineers and the chosen studio facilities.

Many top producers will dictate exactly how the recording sessions should be run, insisting on particular studios, particular staff and particular musicians. Some producers will only ever work in their own studios, which means they get not just the producer's fee but also a payment for the use of their facilities. In other words, top producers can wield a considerable amount of power over both artist and record company.

Home studios

The home studio is a comparatively recent phenomenon, made possible by improved technologies which have allowed equipment to become more compact and cheaper. Many artists, composers and producers today have their own studios; some only ever use them as glorified notepads, rushing down the garden, up into the attic or down into the cellar whenever an idea comes to them, and getting it down on tape in demo form to be worked on later.

Many producers are finding that using their own home studios can make a production budget go a lot further. Laying down basic tracks in a home studio can save money which might be better spent on a professional studio for the final mix of a record. Increasingly these days, it is the final mix – the process during which already recorded instruments and voices are blended together, balanced, multitracked and embellished with effects – which determines how a record will sound to the consumer.

However, few producers will be able to afford professional or even semiprofessional-standard home studios at the early stages of their careers. The home studio is a luxury that will come with time and a certain amount of success.

THE PRODUCER AND THE ENGINEER: WHAT'S THE DIFFERENCE?

Basically, the engineer does what the producer says. That's the simplest way of defining the two roles. If a producer wants a certain sound, he or she will ask the engineer to create the right electronic and acoustic environment in order that it can be achieved. To take two extreme examples of the producer–engineer relationship, there are those producers who will effectively do all the engineering themselves and there are those who will never so much as touch a fader. So, the former will set up the studio, oversee the sound checks and balances and run the desk during both the recording and the mixing sessions. The latter, on the other hand, will concentrate on the theory only and leave the practical work as described above to the engineer.

Therefore, the job of sound engineer clearly offers the best training for the more senior post of producer.

Today, with financial resources becoming ever scarcer, producer–engineers are becoming increasingly common. These people have to combine the abilities of both jobs and may come from either a musical or an engineering background.

Becoming an engineer

The qualifications required to become an engineer vary, depending on what area of music most interests you. A classical sound engineer would usually require a degree in music, simply to demonstrate an understanding of the music and its make-up.

To work in the 'rock' or 'pop' fields, the degree wouldn't usually be necessary. A minimum of four or five GCSEs (including English and maths) and some demonstrated musical ability would often be all that's required, your passion, creative urge and demonstrated desire to live, eat and breathe recording studio equipment 24 hours a day, being as important as your academic qualifications.

As an assistant engineer, you will work with the senior engineer throughout the recording and mixing process, and from this position will be able to gain invaluable knowledge about what the engineer's and producer's jobs entail. If, after a while, you remain convinced that the producer's job is for you, then all you have to do is prove it!

Becoming a producer

There are many routes to the job of record producer and few have attained the position simply by acquiring the right qualifications. You will need more than perfect pitch and a qualification from the Royal Academy of Music to win the trust of a bunch of temperamental, egotistical and, sometimes, very rich and powerful artists. Going back once again to Brian Eno, U2 didn't beg him to work with them (how many people do U2 ever have to *beg* to?) because of his qualifications. It was for a million other things, the combination of which only exists in Brian Eno.

Eno became a producer after some success as an artist, for example as Roxy Music's first keyboard player. He has also written and recorded his own solo work and, most important, written for and produced other artists. Eno's creative use of electronics, recorded sound and acoustics and his unique ability to hear in a song or a recorded piece of music an infinite number of things that others would never hear are what makes him a producer in demand.

George Martin, on the other hand, acquired his reputation initially on the strength of the work he had done with The Beatles, and there will be artists today who would still want him on that basis and on that basis alone. Martin earned his wings pre-Beatles, however, as a graduate of the Guildhall School of Music and later as a freelance (or session) oboe player. He was subsequently recommended to Parlophone, one of EMI's smaller labels, by one of the professors at the Guildhall.

Most top-name producers have become so via a reputation for some other related craft. Tony Visconti, perhaps best known for the albums he produced for David Bowie, was a musician on the New York scene who wandered from rock to jazz. Back in the early sixties, still young and disenchanted with much of what he was hearing on the radio, he decided to make his own tapes and put them around various record companies in the hope of a deal. It worked to a limited extent, but it was the tapes and the way they'd been put together, with his wife in the couple's home studio, which eventually attracted the attention of a record company bigwig. With his musical background as a performer in various styles (excelling at the double bass) and as one who could read music and had a demonstrated skill at making recordings, he was offered a producer's job by the then boss of RCA Records, with whom he had released a handful of singles. The rest, as they say, is history, which records a list of credits on work by Bowie, Marc Bolan, Thin Lizzy and Bob Geldof's Boomtown Rats.

A more formal route?

There are courses of study you can follow which would go some way in preparing you for the job (Appendix B), but it is rare that anyone would step out of such a course and straight into the position of producer, however well you might have qualified. The BA Hons in pop music/recording (which requires five GCSEs and two A-levels or four GCSEs and three A-levels) would prepare you well for the producer's job, but it is unlikely that it would be sufficient on its own without a recommendation or introduction from a respected member of the industry.

A less formal route

Investing in a portable studio (there are various makes on the market) and some basic equipment, begging a spare room from friends or relatives and offering to record/produce local bands' demos for free is not a bad way to start out. Such experience will particularly give you a head start with the diplomacy skills referred to earlier.

Technological developments, such as sampling and other computer techniques, have allowed a whole new sector to develop within the music business. Such technology can be quite cheaply acquired and can allow recordings to be made in a bedroom or garage with very few instruments and at very low cost. Thus, a new breed of producer has been born, creating tracks primarily aimed at a club audience which draw heavily on repetitive beats and a whole range of sampled ingredients.

There are many such artist–producers around, and the best always float to the top and get noticed. There are a number of producers around today who can command high fees and top-name acts, yet who came originally from this cottage-industry sector of the business.

DAYS IN THE LIFE OF THE PRODUCER

If a producer has been signed to a major, big-budget album (total budget, say, £250 000 or more), his or her life is very likely to change dramatically for a period of several months, during which time the artists concerned, a bunch of session musicians and the management of all concerned live and breathe little else. Here's how this time could be divided up:

- After signing the deal, the producer might spend several hours or even days with the manager of the artist or band concerned, learning all about the musical likes, dislikes and preferences of the creative people involved. At this point, management and A&R will talk about the sort of album they hope will come from these recording sessions. At this stage, or before, the producer might also study past recordings made by the band.

- The producer may well know the musicians he or she is about to record. Some have been with particular artists or bands for so long that many of these early formalities can be bypassed. A producer new to the act, however, will want to get to know them and the new material they have prepared for this album. Ideally, informal discussions about the proposed songs and how the band envisages them sounding will take place before producer and artists go into the studio. This will not only help give the producer an idea of what's expected of him or her, but will also help all concerned to get to know and, hopefully, like each other.

- The producer will now take the information gleaned from these pre-studio meetings and start considering which engineer (or engineers), session musicians, instruments and studio (or studios) should be used. The manager, A&R department or the act to be recorded may have stipulated who should be used in the contract signed by the producer. Otherwise, there will be those whom the producer favours. If you regularly check producer credits on vinyl albums or CDs, you will notice that many producers take particular session musicians with them from job to job.

- It is in the studio that a good producer will demonstrate his or her true worth. If a session goes well it will not only be because the artists have performed well, but also because the chosen studio suited all concerned; the chosen engineer worked sympathetically with all concerned; session people turned up on time; songs were properly and effectively interpreted to the satisfaction of the writers and everybody was happy with the final product, which was completed without going over budget. If all this does happen, it will largely be down to the producer; and if it happens time after time with the same producer at the helm then that producer will be able not only to command higher and higher fees but also to choose, to an extent, the calibre of artist he or she works with.

WHEN YOU GET THERE

If you are determined that it is the producer's job you want, then once you get there the rewards are considerable. Not only do you get to be involved in your artists' creative process, often as a key element in the recording process and the finished product, but you are spared much of the discomfort and lack of privacy which goes with the job of being a high-profile touring artist.

You can make rock star-type money as a producer too. Some share in *all* the profits made by an artist, whether or not they are earned directly from a recording in which they were involved. And even if you never strike such a favourable deal, a percentage share in a big-selling album is never to be sniffed at.

9

Marketing a release

Marketing is a term which has gained respectability within the music business in recent years.

During the sixties and into the seventies, artists particularly worked to perpetuate the myth that, if a record was good, it would sell itself, and that to promote it through advertising and other artificial means was simply to devalue the work of art.

It would be nice to think that was true; it's not nice hearing people talking about 'product' when they mean 'record' or even 'song'; it's not nice to hear people speak of 'target groups' or 'consumers' when they mean 'people', 'fans' or 'audience'. But over the past 10 years the marketing of records has become an important part of the work of a record company, and the people who do it need to be dispassionate about the 'product' they are selling. Otherwise, each marketing strategy would be based, in part, on the whims and preferences of the people in the marketing department, and this would not be fair on those acts which didn't find favour with the marketing people. To take a few steps back from the artist and the music means that a clearer marketing strategy can be applied, and that should be beneficial to everyone concerned.

In fact, there has always been marketing; it simply wasn't always called that. When Brian Epstein put The Beatles in their grey suits and when Andrew Loog Oldham put The Rolling Stones in theirs, these were marketing decisions on the part of these two managers, subtly different marketing decisions too. The Beatles' suits were about respectability and uniformity, while The Stones' were more about foppery, sleaze and sex – they were specifically designed to accentuate the boys' bottoms. Target audiences were clearly in mind even then.

A little later, in the spaced-out seventies when some bands (notably Led Zeppelin) were refusing to provide their record company with the ultimate marketing tool, the single, others were benefiting from the application of marketing tactics. John Gaydon, who managed Marc Bolan in the early days, tells of how a simple decision turned the diminutive Bolan from a misunderstood hippy poet into a camp rock and roll monster. Bolan used to sit down and play his songs and no one would take any notice. One day it was suggested that he stood up. He did so and never looked back.

Nowadays the science of music marketing is more exact and better understood and therefore can be applied to lesser known artists. What this does mean, however, is that if enough time and money is spent on a particular act it can be afforded a higher profile than perhaps its talent and material can sustain. This is one of the reasons for the increase in the number of acts which appear to rise to the top with considerable speed but which then disappear as quickly. Clever marketing can get you there but it can't always keep you there.

THE MARKETING STRATEGY

Recording is nearing completion: a single is to be released, and the album from which it is taken will follow. It's now time to work out how to sell these products, and this will ultimately be the responsibility of the record company marketing department under the marketing director.

The nature of a marketing campaign is determined largely by the status of the act in question. A big act means a big marketing budget; a small (new or low-selling) act means a small marketing budget. Some new acts will be afforded a budget far greater than that of other unknowns simply because they have been earmarked as *top priority* by the record company. This could simply be because the signs are that this is, for some reason, a very special act. It might otherwise be because the act fits into a category which is faring well on the national and international markets at a particular moment. In other words, if there has been a spate of successful blonde, teenage female dance artists (for example), a record company might simply wish to *position* its newly discovered offering in this category right up there with the others. This will require a costly marketing campaign which will allow the unknown to assume instant star status. Expensive videos, glossy press advertisements and high-profile radio and television appearances will be required, and all of this will cost money. And such an investment will not always pay off. Such *hype* is always risky but has clearly worked a sufficient number of times for the record companies to want to keep at it.

So, the budget is set according to the artist and the work begins on the marketing strategy. There are three broad elements to any artist/recording marketing strategy: the image, the target group and the timing. We'll start with the image.

The image

An artist's image has to be decided upon very early in the day because all marketing materials, from posters to concert tickets, from videos to stage outfits, depend upon it. Many artists will refuse to be styled, in other words have an image carved out for them which is then reinforced in every bit of printed and filmed matter which pertains to the particular recording or event which is being marketed. In the prevailing antimarketing atmosphere of the early seventies, key exponents of the philosophy would have resisted having clothes and hairstyles chosen for them and would have attempted to make a virtue of their resistance to such superficiality. Fewer artists resist being styled these days, and many positively love the whole process; some even take control of the process themselves.

It is important to remember that styling is not a new idea. Although individuals, even whole companies, making fortunes from designing and styling the stars is a comparatively recent phenomenon, people have been influencing, and even creating, the 'look' of a particular act since the early sixties and even before that time. What, after all, was the most talked-about aspect of The Beatles' image in the early days? Their hairstyles. These hairstyles were based on a style given to *fifth* Beatle Stu Sutcliffe by his girlfriend, German art student Astrid Kirchherr, who the *moptops* (so-named after those haircuts) met in Germany. Today Kirchherr plays down her role in styling The Beatles, but it is true to say that if Sutcliffe hadn't had the hairstyle then George

Harrison and, somewhat more reluctantly Lennon and McCartney, would not have followed suit. Legend has it that John Lennon was the last to agree to wash the grease out of his short back and sides and comb it forward. What the hairstyles did for the band, their international profiles and notoriety, however, is indisputable, whether Lennon liked the idea or not.

So, these days, what Astrid Kirchherr did perhaps unwittingly people are making fortunes from. And if we take an image such as George Michael's black-leather-jacketed look, which he sported at the time the *Faith* album was released, and throughout the *Faith* tour, it is clear to see how effective such styling can be. Shot in close-up on the *Faith* album sleeve, the George-Michael-as-James-Dean image was a strong one. The image reappeared for the *Faith* video (complete with blue jeans and sunburst semi-acoustic guitar), was stamped on the tickets for the *Faith* tour and when the time came to play the title track of the album on stage Michael got into the gear, struck a pose with the very same guitar and even made verbal reference to the *look* during the song's introduction. *Faith* sold over 13 million copies worldwide. And while one could never prove that it was ever anything but the music which sold that album, what was important to *Faith's* international campaign was to have a simple image, in this case that of the leather-jacketed rock 'n' roller, that would mean something all over the world.

The stylist

Styling no longer happens in the random way in which it happened to The Beatles in those early days. At the early stages of a marketing campaign today, all those involved in the visual aspects of an act will come together to ensure that the artist's chosen image is coordinated throughout the marketing campaign (see below). The image may be born out of a photo shoot. An artist may choose a favourite photographer to shoot album cover shots, publicity shots to be sent out to magazines and newspapers and the main poster shots, if a poster campaign is to form part of the wider marketing strategy.

This photo shoot could well define *the look* for the whole of the campaign which surrounds a tour and the album and singles it is intended to promote. The artist, the subject of this shoot, will in many cases be dressed and made up by a stylist

(Chapter 10). The stylist might provide clothes as requested by the artist, in other words employ clothes designers and hair-dressers of the artist's choosing, or may be trusted by the artist to come up with the right choices. The stylist's work may cross over into videos, which will most likely be shot after publicity stills, posters and album covers, but which may well have to coordinate with all of the above. So the stylist plays a crucial role, defining the look, and ensuring that it satisfies the artist, the marketing people, the management, A&R and, most importantly, the fans.

The target group

It is well publicized that *Faith* was the tool with which George Michael decided finally to lay to rest his teens-only image. So again it was important that the *Faith* look meant something to the new, more mature audience he was now targeting, as well as to the die-hard swooning teenage fans. A young man clad in jeans and leather is an image tried and tested with young pop fans the world over, so he had a winner there. Meanwhile, older audiences would appreciate the switch from the suntanned Club 18 – 30 image which dominated the Wham! years, to something they recognized as very much a fifties' image (Elvis, James Dean) though more recently reinvented by the likes of Bruce Springsteen. And of course the Americans, to whom Wham! had never properly broken through, would particularly relate to this classic look.

This was a simple image, which would do the job across a wide audience. Michael had a large hand in the creation of this image, although once created it then becomes the task of the marketing department to coordinate its use.

In the case of *Faith*, the target groups were broad, and so a careful but far-reaching press campaign would be employed. Advertising would be more carefully targeted – advertisements in magazines aimed at an older rock and roll audience such as *Rolling Stone* and *Q* would be obvious choices; teen magazines such as *Smash Hits* would no longer be enough. Better, perhaps, to advertise in the newspapers read by parents (mothers particularly?) of the younger George Michael fans, so as to reach them second hand via the people who, after all, are going to be funding the album and ticket purchases. And if the younger members of the family have gone off George, then perhaps parents might develop an interest instead. After all, he must be OK: he advertised in their paper, didn't he?

The timing

All the above, from deciding upon the image to the placing of the right ad in the right paper or on the right TV channel, is the responsibility of the marketing department, which works under the marketing director. The process will begin, as the recording and mixing of an album draws to a close, with a meeting of the marketing department, the artist's management and usually the artist. Here all aspects of the marketing campaign will be discussed, from how the artist will be *packaged* for photography, press interviews and television appearances, to where advertising, if any, will be placed.

At this point in the proceedings, it might be decided that an outside PR company (Chapter 11) and possibly even an outside marketing company might be brought in to steer the campaign. This would be done for one of the following reasons:

- The artist/management company concerned favours a particular marketing company and has the sway/budget to persuade the record company to use that company.

- The artist concerned is so big that the record company's marketing department is simply not big enough to cope with the job in hand.

- The artist's music is of a particular genre in which there are several specialized marketing/PR companies operating.

- The artist/management company owns a marketing/PR company and insists that it is used.

If outside people are used to steer the campaign, this will always be done in collaboration with the record company's marketing director who, for example, will set and control the budgets and approve work as the campaign proceeds.

The campaign will involve photographs to distribute to press and to use on album sleeves, posters, concert programmes, etc. The photographer will most likely be chosen by artist or management, and photos will be approved by all parties. Posters, sleeves, labels and press advertisements will then have to be ordered, and their delivery must be timed so that they reach their destinations to coincide with the release of the album, single or album and single.

If there is a single, a video has to be made (Chapter 10). Again, in the case of well-established artists, the choice of video production company and director will be theirs, in collaboration with management. In the case of a new unknown, presuming a video is made at all, the record company will have a strong hand in the choice of production company, and much of this decision will be based on (the very small) budget available.

Excerpts from the video might well be used later in any television advertising which might become part of the marketing strategy, so timing the delivery of the video will also be crucial.

Anyone who has seen a record company department or an independent marketing company at work during the run-up to a new campaign will perhaps wonder why everyone is screaming at each other, why everything is timed to the last minute, why printers run late, why artwork is never delivered on time, why nobody ever seems to have the time to sit down and talk to anyone and, most bewildering of all, why it always seems to work in the end.

The answer to all these questions is that none of the avenues open to an artist for publicity and promotion, such as page space in a magazine, television ad slots, radio ad slots, television and radio interview slots, concert halls for promotional tours, poster space in retail outlets and appearances on music shows, children's shows and breakfast and daytime television shows, can ever be booked very far in advance. To take an extreme example: it would be madness to book the Albert Hall a year in advance of the completion and release of an album. How can you know the album will be ready? How can you know it will be any good? How do you know that the band (if it is a band) will still be together by then? And if it is still together, how can you know it will still be popular?

The nature of the popular music business (unlike classical, where everything is more predictable although, ironically, comparatively little is ever spent on marketing) is that it is up to the minute, and therefore everything that is done around it tends to be up to the minute. So to work in the marketing department of a record company, or an independent marketing company, you will need to be of sound constitution, have a thick skin, have little social life (around the time of a campaign at least) and be totally dedicated to your job.

The charts

One of the primary goals of a marketing department is to get a single into the charts. And here timing is crucial. There are only a few weeks after a single's release in which to do this, because if a single hangs around too long the people with the power to get it into the charts – radio producers, DJs and the retailers – will give up on it. Once a single is in the charts, however, marketing becomes a lot easier, as a chart placing will guarantee some TV exposure, on MTV and chart-oriented programmes, and the record will stand a very good chance of being included in most radio playlists (Chapter 12). Once a single makes the charts, retailers will be much more interested in stocking the album when it comes out. If the album is already out, a charting single usually means repeat orders for that album, as the single will have given it a second wind.

A single or an album gets into the charts on the strength of the speed of sales. If a single sells 20 000 copies in 1 week in the UK, for example, it is likely to achieve a high position in the national singles chart, depending upon how many other high-selling singles there are around at that time. If it were to sell 20 000 copies over 30 weeks, on the other hand, its chart position could be negligible. So that initial rush of sales is all-important and in many cases is what the marketing strategy is geared towards.

National singles charts are becoming less important than they used to be, however, and this is because singles sales have continued to drop off since the introduction of the CD and the beginning of the growth of the computer games market and the introduction of 'console' game systems in the late eighties. In the spring of 1994 the UK's biggest record retailer, Woolworth, stopped selling vinyl singles altogether. Such was the importance of the charts at one time, however, that serious crimes were committed so that certain singles achieved a high placing.

National singles and album charts are compiled on the basis of weekly sales returns from a selection of record shops around the country, a system clearly open to corruption. The retailing industry and the record companies will say that the manipulation of the charts doesn't happen as much these days. But then they would say that, wouldn't they? (The UK's two major national record charts are those compiled by the Market Research Information Bureau (MRIB) and used by the music papers the *NME* and *Melody Maker* and the ITV *Teletext* service, and The UK Charts, compiled by Millward Brown Market Research Ltd for the Chart Information Network (CIN) and used by the BBC. Both sets of charts are based solely on sales returns.)

THE JOBS

In a small indie there may be no marketing department. The job might be coordinated by the A&R manager or even the managing director, or handled on behalf of the record company by the artist's management. In a big company, on the other hand, there will most definitely be a marketing department, and the size of that department will depend on the size of the company.

Whatever its size, the marketing department's job is principally one of liaison: with designers (who may or may not be in-house); printers (who definitely won't be in-house); press, PR and promoters (who may or may not be in-house); the artist and the artist's management; newspaper, magazine, radio and television advertising sales departments; and upwards with the marketing director and, beyond him or her, with the managing director and/or president of the record company.

To be employed within an independent marketing company which works specifically within the music business, or within a record company marketing department, you will most likely need a marketing qualification of some sort (Appendix B). You may also have to demonstrate a knowledge of current trends, either through an easily substantiated passion for and knowledge of the music scene or through recent experience with another record company, an artist's management company, a plugging company (Chapter 12) or a record retailer. Experience of, or qualifications in, design might also help you here.

In a very large company, one of the big multinationals such as Sony or EMI for example, where the marketing department will be large, marketing and management qualifications would probably take priority over any musical experience or knowledge you might have, particularly if you were aiming for a management position within the department.

10

Video

It was December 1975 when bands, songwriters, producers and record companies in Britain were to learn exactly how important the video or *pop promo* was going to be to the record industry. For it was in that month that the rock group Queen began its nine-week run at the top of the UK singles chart with the epic single Bohemian Rhapsody.

The epic single came with an epic video, a video, made for just £5000, which is widely credited not just for keeping the single at the top of the charts for such a long time, but also for persuading the music industry that videos sell records.

This is the first and most important point to consider when contemplating entering the music video side of the record industry: a video is an advertisement, a promotional tool to be used by the record company and artist as part of a marketing strategy. The video may be considered an art form by some, but as far as the record industry is concerned the video is primarily a marketing tool. Sensitive artists need not apply!

The video does represent a considerable proportion of the creative input that goes into the success of a single, however, which in turn may serve to sell an album. Bohemian Rhapsody is a good case in point. It was a stunning record, with an equally impressive video. Whether or not the record company executives considered it to be little more than a marketing tool, the fact that it was a striking and original piece of work was crucial to its effectiveness.

There are other examples in which a video made a considerable contribution to the fortunes of a single. Take the case of arguably two of the world's greatest ever rock stars, Paul McCartney and Michael Jackson. One of their joint efforts, the 1983 single Say, Say, Say, was not doing as well over in the UK as a collaboration by two such stars should. A video starring the two singers had been made, for the exorbitant sum of $500 000, but in the UK there were few outlets for it to be shown. (MTV existed in the US by this time, but not in Europe.) True, there was *Top of the Pops*, but the show's then strict rules allowed only rising Top 40 singles to be featured. Say, Say, Say was on its way down the chart.

Keen for the impressive video to be seen, McCartney uncharacteristically agreed to a live weekday early evening television interview during which the video by director Bob Giraldi would be discussed and played. Sure enough, this reversed the fortunes of the song, which eventually made it to number two in the UK charts. In the US, where the video had enjoyed considerably more exposure, it reached number one.

The year 1983 marked the peak of video's silly period, during which budgets were rising and their 'premières' were becoming media events. Michael Jackson's *Thriller* video was first shown in full on MTV in the US on 2 December, 1983. The build-up to the broadcast was of the type normally reserved for a major sports event. But then this was no ordinary video. A new version of the song had been created especially for it, which included an extended version of the song's rap performed by the late horror movie actor Vincent Prince; top US film director Jon Landis was brought in to direct, and a budget of over $2m was allocated to the film, the finished version of which ran to 15 minutes.

This video, of course, did its job. The album's sales rocketed as the video won more and more television exposure worldwide, and remains unbeaten to this day as the world's biggest selling album ever. But the video was to be the last of its kind. Never again was so much money spent on a single video.

The eighties' excesses now behind us, it is unlikely that the budget for any video will ever reach even a fifth of that of *Thriller*. But if you consider that the average video director will earn 10% of a video's budget, it is still clear to see what attracts people to the job.

As video budgets rose and the number of videos being produced increased during those years, so a lot of young people began to make sums of money they had not even dreamed of. In the chic media-dominated London of the early eighties, video companies were springing up alongside the spanking new design studios and advertising agencies which also boomed during that time, all of them typified by designer furniture inside and stylishly understated shop fronts and clamped classic cars outside.

The excessive eighties didn't come to an end without leaving a few casualties behind. Many of those classic cars were repossessed along with the designer furniture as recession-hit companies started to go bust, and in the video business many went bust unnecessarily because to set yourself up as a video producer or director, you need little more than a desk and a telephone. Expensive offices need to be paid for even when the business isn't coming in and that is the lesson that many learned the hard way when the video boom came to an end.

But surely you need more than that? What about staff, cameras, lighting and editing equipment? Or at least, what about somewhere to put your desk and telephone?

Office premises can be a help, they certainly serve to create a professional working environment. But then even some bands these days work out of their bedrooms. The point here is that the video business, like so many other media services, exists almost entirely using freelance people. Here's how the business works.

FIRST, YOU NEED A SINGLE

Chapters elsewhere in this book take us to the point at which the single has been made. Surrounding that single there will be a marketing strategy, and central to that strategy is the video.

Most record companies employ somebody whose task it is to commission videos. This person can be called by a number of titles, for example commissioning editor for video or head of video. Alternatively the job might be done as a one-off by the A&R person attached to the artist (Chapter 7), or by even the artist's management (Chapter 4). For the sake of this chapter, let's refer to this person as the commissioning editor.

The commissioning editor will have to be aware of who's in and who's out where today's video directors are concerned.

When the time comes for a video for a single to be made (usually just prior to release, but sometimes after), the commissioning editor will contact between three and six directors whom he or she regards as appropriate for the artist in question with a request to see their showreels, a sort of visual CV. The showreels will give the best examples of these directors' past works, and the artist and management will study them before deciding which directors to approach.

The directors will then be sent a tape of the single and asked to write a treatment for a video to accompany the track. The treatment will, in no more than a page and a half, describe what happens in the video and how it will look. Artist and management will then study the treatments before deciding on which lucky director gets the job.

Then, before work starts, it is down to the commissioning editor and the production company that employs the director (more on the production company/producer later in this chapter) to settle on a budget. A contract is then drawn up between record company and production company. The terms of this contract, which will have been checked over by the lawyers of both parties, will be adhered to throughout the video production process.

WHO PAYS, AND WHO EARNS WHAT?

Once the commissioning editor, artist's management and artist have settled on a director, it is the responsibility of the video producer to sort out the logistics of the video shoot, and that has to start with money. No multimillion dollar videos are made any more; a sensible budget for a reasonably well-known artist might be between £30 000 and £50 000. A big name – Elton John, U2, Gloria Estefan, Guns'n'Roses, for example – might go over the £100 000 mark and even creep towards £200 000, although such figures are rare these days.

Whatever the budget agreed, it's the record company that pays, and that budget is subsequently controlled by the producer, who now begins the task of getting the video made. Here, incidentally, is the basic difference between the producer and the director: the producer oversees the making of the video; the director (with crew) actually makes it.

As far as payments are concerned, these are also agreed at the start. Typically, the director will earn around 10% of the budget; the producer, 5%. If our imaginary video costs £50 000, the lucky director gets £5 000 and the producer £2 500. Given that a video rarely takes more than 2 weeks to make from start to finish (including editing, but excluding negotiations which include settling on an idea) that's pretty good money. It's unlikely, however, that any one director will be making video after video throughout the year. Ten in a year is pretty good going; the big money that can be made when there is work around makes up for the times when there isn't any.

There's £42 500 left for getting our imaginary video made. Except that out of this there will also be a fee to be paid to the video production company simply to cover overheads and by way of a commission payment for its role in assembling the talent for the video.

THE PRODUCTION COMPANY

The video production company serves as a base from which directors and producers can operate their business. Typically, few creative staff will be permanently employed; more likely, the company will be owned and headed by a producer or executive producer, who will cultivate a stable of freelance producers and directors who will be called upon as work turns up. Any permanent staff will work mainly on the administration side.

Such production companies work almost like talent agencies; the record company's commissioning editor (or an artist or artist's management) will become familiar with certain companies, will have favourites and will be more likely to use favourite people than to seek out new producers and directors from scratch, knowing that their favourite production companies will indirectly be doing that seeking out for them, all year round.

Few production companies survive entirely on videos alone. That used to be possible in the eighties but today it's important for a production company to diversify, and this has been made easier by the changes to the television industry which, conveniently, coincided with the great video crash of the mid to late eighties.

Today, all of the UK's broadcasters 'commission out' a proportion of their programming, rather than making it all themselves;

Channel 4, for example, commissions all of its programmes from independent production companies, making it a publisher–broadcaster rather than a broadcaster and programme maker.

This gives video production companies the opportunity to diversify into making television programmes. Often it can work the other way around, the established independent television production companies occasionally diversifying into pop and rock videos.

Such flexibility is good news for the directors, producers and crew members, who may have ambitions beyond what they're doing. If you succeed as a video director working within the framework of a production company which also makes television programmes, the opportunities for sidestepping into the television business are there for the taking.

WHO DOES WHAT?

The commissioning editor

All record companies now have a video department; it may exist within the creative services department (Chapter 3), and within this department there will be a person or people whose job it is to commission videos for new singles. The video department will be in constant contact with the marketing and A&R departments (video may simply be a part of the marketing department), which together will keep the video department informed on how a new act is progressing and when a video to promote a single will most likely be required. The video department staff will in the meantime be in touch with developments in the world of independent production companies so that when a video is required they know exactly who to go to.

Budgets will most likely be dictated to the video department by the A&R department, in conjunction with the artist's management. The record company will pay for the video, but the money will most likely be deducted from the artist's advance or future royalties or a combination of both. The artist's manager will want to keep an eye on the final source of the cash.

The director

The director is the creative person who comes up with the ideas which eventually end up on screen and who will often choose the more 'creative' people in the crew, the art director, the lighting camera operator (see below) and the stylist, for example. The director will guide actors, artists and camera crew on location, and will basically be responsible for the final look of the video, which will come together at the editing stage. The producer will allocate a budget to the director and, while the producer is clearly the money person, it is very much the director's job to stay within budget. Flights of creative fancy cost money.

The producer

The producer is the level-headed organizer who controls cash, gets the crew together in collaboration with the director and is basically responsible for delivering the final product to the record company – on time and within budget. It's a satisfying but thankless task, because in many ways the producer is seen as the baddie of the bunch, the person who says 'no' to more money, 'no' to more time and 'I'm sorry it's late' to the record company. Get a reputation as a no-hassle producer who delivers good product on time and never overspends, however, and you've a job for life.

The lighting-camera operator

This is the director's right-hand person who can interpret what the director wants through the camera lens and on to the film/videotape and ultimately on to the screen. A director can have the most creative ideas imaginable, but if this person can't capture them on film they're worthless.

The art director

Sets and locations have to be realized in accordance with the director's ideas. The art director works with the stylist, lighting camera operator and director to create the backdrops for the film.

The stylist

The stylist's job is to take the producer's money and go clothes shopping with a bunch of rock stars to ensure that they look good on screen. The stylist will also buy props, and dress the artists (and sometimes the set) in collaboration with the art director. On occasions, the two jobs become one. But aspiring stylists beware: not all artists are beautiful, kind and friendly; some are unfriendly, look dreadful and will give you a hard time if you don't make them look otherwise. The job can be great fun, but diplomacy is often required.

The editor

The editor is the person who takes the reels of film and cuts them down to 3 minutes' worth of sexy footage designed to make the artist look as exciting as possible, thus helping the record to sell. The editor should ideally have a strong musical sense and, in a perfect world, wouldn't wait in the editing suite for the rolls of film to arrive, but would get out there on location to advise the director what might cut together and what won't.

Special effects

In many other areas of the music industry, there are those who argue that new technologies formats such as digital compact cassette (DCC) and minidisc, along with digital radio are serving to kill some elements of the music business. In the case of video, however, new technologies are likely to be its saviour. Special effects technologies have created a whole new layer of skills which can be applied to the business of making videos. There are also the new interactive technologies which are likely to serve the maker of music videos well in the future.

Supporting roles

There are many jobs on video crews which don't make the headlines – production assistants, assistant directors (not often used on video shoots), focus pullers, clapper-loaders and runners all play an essential part in the making of a video. Those who play these supporting roles get noticed fast because there's no slacking on a video shoot. The job has to be done fast, and anyone sitting around and there for the hell of it will be spotted and won't be asked back. Similarly, even if you're there carrying out a seemingly menial task, do it well and your potential will be noted, and this will be the best route to the job you're really after.

There are many examples of runners making it big in the business. Runners are the fit young men and women you might see sprinting across towns and cities with film cans under their arms or poking out of their back packs, whose job it is to rush the finished reels of film to and from the processors so that work can be constantly monitored. It is an important if badly paid role, but one which will reveal a person's worth, willingness and talent in a very short time.

GETTING INTO THE BUSINESS

The commissioning editor

When applying for a job commissioning videos for a record company it will be important to be able to demonstrate a knowledge of the existing outlets for video, the purpose of a video and how it fits into the marketing strategy for an album or single, the importance of an artist's image and knowledge of how a video is made.

This person will either have come up from within the record company, possibly from the creative services department or the marketing department (Chapter 9), or will have gained some knowledge of video, production budgets, production companies, directors and their styles from elsewhere. The commissioning editor might previously have worked for a video production company as a production assistant.

On the production side

Obvious routes in are via film school or art college or one of various media production courses, although not all will be of help to those aspiring to the pop video business. It is also important not to wait until you're qualified before approaching artists, record companies or production companies. Once you're on a course, be it a general foundation course or studying a particular skill, if music video is what you want to do you should be making your approaches while you're studying.

Commissioning editors and producers will be impressed by anyone who has taken the trouble to produce their own showreel. Do so by getting to know a local band or artist and persuading them to allow you to film them. At this stage, it's not the technical quality that matters as much as the ideas. Prove that you can interpret a song and realize that interpretation on film or video and you're on your way. Beg or borrow (but don't steal) the equipment from colleges, even from hardware manufacturing companies, if you've got the nerve. A standard camcorder would do.

Then, get your showreel seen by artist management companies, record company video departments and independent producers. Always contact the companies first and find the name of the person to whom you should send your tape. Remember, a person-to-person meeting will always be most effective, although few will admit to having the time to see you on the strength of a cold telephone call. Remember, also, if someone does agree to see you to take care to ensure that their intentions are honourable! Late night meetings down dark alleyways or in out-of-the-way apartments or hotel rooms should be avoided. Nobody needs to meet in such conditions, and you should be suspicious of anyone who suggests that you do.

Even the biggest bands will take an unsolicited idea seriously. A true fan can usually second guess an artist's plans for the next single. If you've got the album, you can usually tell what the next single is going to be. Once you've done so, where's the harm in scripting a video for it? Try creating a rough *storyboard* and a short treatment and package them along with any sample work you might have from school or college, or your own amateur videos or photographs, and send it to the artist or artist's manager concerned.

Arguably the world's biggest band (it would be unfair to mention the name) had one such unsolicited proposal in its short list of two for a video in 1993. Unfortunately, the amateur proposal wasn't chosen, but it got further than other proposals from directors with proven track records.

INTERACTIVE

Before you go off to start work on your video proposals, a word about interactive. It is likely that compact disc interactive (CD-I), CD-ROM and even broadcast interactive, that's interactive television, is going to provide musicians and music video makers with a fresh outlet for their talents. For it is clear that, while there will always be people making rock and pop music, records in all formats are not the multimillion selling mass-market products they used to be.

CD-I and CD-ROM, on the other hand, could serve to stimulate the record-buying public once again by virtue of all the add-ons that vinyl and CD could never offer, such as text, video and still photograph, and, of course, CD-quality audio – all there for viewers to interact with in whatever way they choose. For the creative mind that can see the potential of this medium there is a whole series of new career opportunities available.

THE FINISHED PRODUCT

It is not uncommon for an artist or commissioning editor to reject a video. Few are rejected totally, however. Most common is the situation in which an artist doesn't like a particular shot or series of shots of him or herself and the director (usually through the producer) is asked to reshoot certain sequences. Videos do occasionally get thrown out altogether and another producer brought in to create something better. In such a case it would depend on the original contract between the producer and record company, and why the video was rejected, as to who pays for this costly mistake. If the commissioning editor has made the right choice of producer and director and the budget agreed upon was a sensible one, it's unlikely that the commissioning editor will be held ultimately responsible here.

Perhaps the hardest thing for the makers of a music video to take is the way in which the finished product is put to use. For a start, you don't own the finished video, the record company does, and it may never get shown! If it does get shown it may well be cut short by a children's television presenter. Or it might even be used in a television advertisement for the artist's latest album, or even on a long-form video to be sold in the shops.

But if the artist is a big-name artist, and/or the single in question is a hit, there's no question but that your video will be shown over and over again on a number of television stations around the world, and certainly worldwide on MTV.

Will you win fame from this success? Only from within the industry. You will build a reputation and may even get your own silver, gold or platinum disc if the single's a big success.

There are separate awards for videos, too.

Only in very exceptional circumstances will you get any extra cash for all this exposure your video is getting, however. The greatest value your video will have to you once it's complete is the money you earned and the experience you gained when you made it, plus the fact that it will add to your showreel.

Press and public relations

The job of publicist can appear to be among the easiest and most attractive in the music business because there seems to be so much scope for imaginative and off-the-cuff creativity. The job does not require special academic achievements and the work offers the chance to shine as an individual.

The publicist has regular access to artists and gets ample opportunity to observe their work at close quarters. For some people this may be an appealing bonus, even adding an air of glamour to the working lifestyle. On the other hand, an awe-struck star-gazing publicist tends to be an all-round liability rather than an asset!

Although it is true that many PR people in the industry do have the creatively pleasing opportunity to work directly and closely with the artists they represent, the job is also particularly demanding in a number of ways and has a fair bit of stress and tension attached to it.

WHAT SORT OF JOB IS IT?

There is no typical day in the life of a publicist and, if that sounds more like a hell than a joy, this job may not be for you. Priorities overtake and supersede one another hour by hour during the publicist's day, just as they do in the newsroom of a daily newspaper. Urgency and pressure are essential elements of the job and if these tend to stimulate and invigorate you and provide a positive challenge, please read on.

The working day may begin at home with an unexpected fax or phone call about a breaking news story in which a client plays some part. The publicist makes hasty arrangements to join the client somewhere on the far side of town or even a longer car, train or plane journey away from home. Instead of heading for the office, there are changes to be set in motion affecting the rest of the day's timetable – meetings and other routine affairs are postponed to cope with the new emergency. Otherwise, the day that gets under way without such surprises may start with a skim-read of the morning papers. At best, an assistant will have done the skim-read and clipped out stories of special interest.

The mix of the routine day's work might include phone calls to clients and journalists either to talk about specific plans or merely to 'stay in touch', lunch with a particularly useful media contact, a session of press interviews for an artist who has something new to promote and an appointment at a photographer's studio to supervise the shooting of some new publicity pictures. There might be a visit to a magazine editor's office to talk over some story ideas or a trip to a recording studio to meet a new client. There could be a 2-hour conference with record company people to lay the foundations of a whole new PR project. The variations on this theme are endless and, as a rule, almost always add up to a long and busy working day.

The myth which began in Hollywood and has persisted since cinema's golden era is that the showbusiness publicist's job is based on stunts involving celebrities and the invention of sensational but absolutely untrue stories about the stars. The truth is that while Fleet Street used to go along with quite improbable publicists' tales when it suited it, few media editors of the nineties look kindly on blatant PR stunts unless they involve such famous names that publication of a story is likely to sell papers or add viewers.

The publicist needs to have a nose for a promising news story, a well-developed sense of loyalty and discretion, a degree of genuine devotion to the job, the willingness to work crazy hours, plus a wide spread of skills and capabilities, some of which need to be almost instinctive while others are far from easy to learn and cannot be acquired from any textbook or solely via a university or college course.

QUALIFICATIONS OR PERSONALITY?

Quite apart from basic industrial knowledge and a liberal-minded appreciation of music, the publicist requires mental and physical stamina, ingenuity, patience and persistence, a lack of inhibition and a vivacious personality. General intelligence, an ability to communicate without discomfort in both business and social circumstances and hands-on journalistic work experience in some sector of the media count for as much if not more than specialist academic qualifications.

In addition, it helps if the publicist has certain basic office abilities, is able to type and is at least superficially familiar with word processor software, along with the use of a modem and electronic mail.

It is not essential to be able to write to professional journalistic standards but it is useful if the publicist can churn out factually reliable, well-constructed and conveniently presented news stories, company profiles or biographical pieces at reasonable speed and with a high standard of accuracy. Comparatively few publicists farm out to freelance journalists the writing of press releases and other media material. This indicates that at least one person in the average publicist's office is a competent writer.

Various job titles are used to describe more or less the same work: publicist, press officer, public relations consultant, PR account executive, press agent, press representative. For the purposes of this chapter, the word 'publicist' is used, but not for any significant reason.

Over the years, the introduction of new ways of transmitting and delivering information and entertainment to the consumer has broadened the work base of the publicist, who once concentrated on generating press coverage (newspapers and magazines) but now needs to pay equal attention to a wider spectrum of communication media, particularly television and radio. For the publicist, job satisfaction needs to be linked to the volume and quality of positive media exposure gained for the employer or clients.

WHERE TO START

Extremely few independent music publicists set themselves up in business without previous PR experience. The most usual place to acquire that experience is in the press office of a record company.

There are equal job opportunities for women and men in the PR field. If there is an element of bias it may well favour women – some employers and some clients insist that, all other things being equal, women tend to make the more persuasive (and therefore more successful) publicists whether they're dealing with male or female journalists.

In outline, at least, the role of the music business publicist is much the same whether the service is performed as an in-house employee or as an outside independent consultant. Part of the job's appeal is that it has so many parts and the work is seldom repetitive. Each day's activities differ from all others.

WHO EMPLOYS PUBLICISTS?

Artists in all sectors of the music business, from opera to rap, can benefit from press/publicity representation. The launch of an unknown newcomer can use the boost of PR attention to support a first record release or initial public performances. The well-established box-office success and chart-topping recording star with a limited amount of time to spend on interviews and photo sessions needs the expert advice of a publicist over which editorial opportunities to take and which to turn down with minimum loss of goodwill. The greater the artist's celebrity, the more the publicist's role includes an element of protection against unfavourable stories. It is naive to believe that all publicity is good or to underestimate the damage which can be done to an artist's reputation when 'bad press' appears.

In the music business, the largest employers of PR services are the record companies, many of which have their own in-house press offices run by a team of publicists and their assistants. Medium-sized and smaller record companies may not operate a full-blown department but simply employ one or two publicists.

Others who hire full-time publicists or retain the non-exclusive services of independent PR consultants include music publishers, artists' managers/agents, independent record producers and recording studios, music industry associations, concert tour promoters and music video production companies and their distributors. Out-of-house publicists, whether self-employed individuals or part of a consultancy, may be retained on a year-round basis or periodically as and when a client wants a short burst of PR activity to assist in the promotion and marketing of a product, perhaps an album, a tour or a video.

Less frequently, a number of peripheral business interests require the occasional services of a publicist who specializes in music industry accounts. These include film and television producers, clubs (nightclubs, discos, DJs, cabaret rooms), book and specialist magazine publishers, companies providing back-up services for concert tours, merchandising agents and multimedia project 'packagers'.

Whatever specific line of business the music publicist's employer or client is in, an artist or a roster of artists will be at the core of most PR campaigns. Without waiting for others to act on their behalf, individual artists (singers, musicians, bands, composers, compères, television and radio music presenters) often feel that their careers might benefit from a publicity consultant's attention and will approach an independent publicist directly. Such deals can be on a short-term single-campaign basis or can be open-ended. As a rule, if both parties are getting along, the publicist hopes to keep the account indefinitely. The clout of the independent consultant is linked very directly to the strength of his or her client roster and to the attractiveness of the names of those represented in the eyes of media reporters/editors.

THE PUBLICIST'S OFFICE

Whether it is an in-house department or an independent business, the publicist's office set-up will be much the same. The staff will be headed by a senior press officer (or the firm's sole or several owners in the case of an independent consultancy), and there will be one or more press officers (who may be known as PR account executives) and one or more PR assistants and typists. The in-house set-up may share with other departments such office facilities as fax and photocopying machines, whereas the independent publicist carries the full installation and maintenance costs of such essential equipment, along with word processors, printers, etc. Such overheads, together with payroll and office rent, are factors which often persuade the beginner to gain some salaried in-house experience of the job before contemplating the launch of an independent consultancy.

DIVIDED LOYALTIES

The wise publicist's first loyalty lies with those who sign his or her cheques. On the other hand, it is of basic and substantial importance for the publicist to build up and keep a good working relationship with media contacts. Quite frequently publicists face the dilemma of weighing up how far they can afford to upset a valuable journalist in order to please a client, and vice versa.

The minefield of divided loyalties can become even more of a headache whenever influential artists are involved and whenever they become personally concerned with what is happening. An artist's record company, personal manager, music publisher or concert promoter may be paying for the publicist's services, but the artist is quite likely to voice conflicting views over image and the detail of PR strategies. It is a particularly arduous part of the publicist's job to find a mutually amicable compromise.

WHAT SKILLS ARE NEEDED?

Previous journalistic experience is a great asset to anyone contemplating a career in PR, although it should be recognized that not all journalists have the vocational inclination or the right temperament to move into PR. In theory, at least, a journalist who has had regular dealings with publicists should be better equipped to move from one end of the process to the other. While there are no minimum academic qualifications laid down, the average music business publicist will have reached A-level standard of education with examination success in arts subjects and languages, but not necessarily in music.

The publicist must be articulate, have a decent-sized vocabulary, and be a willing and able communicator with an instinctive flair for spotting the makings of an interesting news story or an eye-catching picture. From a ragged jumble of biographical data or a heap of photographer's contact sheets, the publicist should be capable of picking out the tiniest speck of information which might be turned into some sort of media opportunity. Other useful attributes include diplomacy and the ability to respect confidences and keep professional/industrial secrets.

A DEDICATED PROFESSION

Office hours? In a nutshell, forget them! Early in the morning breakfast television/radio reporters and evening newspaper journalists working on first editions may have urgent need to reach a publicist. Similarly, people writing for the final editions of morning papers often work through until midnight or after. So PR work is not for the nine-to-five person. The responsible publicist or a delegated deputy has a duty to remain available to the media 24 hours a day. To be unobtainable during the breaking of a news story concerning a client or employer can be an all-round disaster.

Even when nothing newsworthy is happening, the music business publicist is likely to have great chunks of so-called 'free time' taken up with appointments which blend work with pleasure. There are concerts and receptions to go to, recording studio sessions to attend. On average, the in-house salaried employee gets more clearly defined leisure time than the freelance consultant.

AREAS OF RESPONSIBILITY

Acting as an information source

It is a basic function of the publicist to be thoroughly informed about the activities of the companies and artists he or she represents. Accurate and adequate written information, always kept up to date, should be available to the media on request. Journalists should be able to acquire answers to questions promptly.

It is unprofessional of a publicist not to return calls, even when it is to respond to requests (perhaps for interview or photo facilities) with a negative answer. A negative answer ought to be accompanied by a credible reason or explanation which protects the client's interests as much as possible.

Keeping mailing lists updated

Media contacts change jobs quite frequently, and an out-of-date press office mailing list becomes a less than useful work tool. Although it is often better to send out too many pieces of paper than too few, the astute publicist takes the extra time and trouble to categorize mailing lists into sections to suit different purposes and occasions. If this is done properly, specialist journalists receive targeted material which is relevant to their work, waste is kept to a minimum and press releases reach the right people who can make valuable use of them.

Putting out the news

The publicist needs to know how to construct an instantly attractive news release, sometimes creating a good story from less-than-attractive raw material, putting the vital facts at the top of the copy and the background information lower down. Brevity is as important as accuracy. News, real news, should be delivered by the fastest possible and most efficient method, probably fax or electronic mail.

Image building

Whether acting individually as head of a small independent PR consultancy or within a team of full-time marketing and promotional executives at a major record company, the publicist is very directly concerned with image creation and revision This can involve the design or improvement of a company's overall public image (with the introduction of fresh corporate livery and logo) or the professional image of an artist.

It can be a fascinating challenge for the publicist to start from scratch on the creation, development and establishment of a new artist's image prior to launch. The image of an artist is projected not only via a style or styles of music but also by appearance and personality.

Areas a publicist is likely to enter include definition of musical style, the visual image for photo sessions and public appearances/performances (grooming, hair, clothing), choice of the most suitable media for the occasion (which publications or programmes to go for and which to treat as lower priority or simply avoid) and coordination of design across all the advertising and packaging in a multimedia campaign. A publicist may also become involved in redefining an established artist's image, particularly to coincide with a change of career direction, a new album or fresh series of concerts.

Contributing towards a wider campaign

The publicist generally plays a part in the overall concept of promotional and marketing campaigns, meeting with sales and advertising people to ensure that everyone shares a common knowledge of what is happening and recognizes a common spread of targets.

Corporate affairs

The music industry publicist need not be a specialist in such matters but should have some basic knowledge and understanding of how a company is run and how it wishes to be perceived by outsiders. The publicist often issues corporate news stories based on information provided by a company's business, legal or financial executives. For such occasions, contact with financial/city journalists and business affairs programmes is necessary.

Promotion and protection

Positive promotion of the employer's or client's activities in the public marketplace is the top priority of the publicist. But there are times where a reverse strategy needs to be applied and a different expertise comes into play. Such occasions arise when there is call for damage limitation over a story which threatens to spoil the reputable name of a company or the 'clean' reputation of an artist.

Protective PR know-how includes putting the best possible face on an unfavourable story, perhaps by countering quickly with something positive, and can also mean calling in favours from friendly media contacts. This is where a publicist's diplomatic skills come into play and the strength and level of his or her relationships with media people become important.

Stimulating media interest

Mutual trust between a journalist and a publicist is the best basis for successful business. Wining and dining media contacts as a means of developing or consolidating relationships is fine, but the wise publicist delays 'hard-sell' discussion of specific stories until another occasion rather than pushing specific stories between courses. Many prefer to avoid 'hard-sell' tactics altogether, knowing that there are few people journalists dislike more intensely than the time-consuming ear-bending publicist who hopes that sheer brute-force verbal assault will compensate for a weak case. The publicist's task is to present the facts in a persuasive way, but not to press a case too zealously or aggressively and cause irritation. Two-way cooperation beats unilateral brute force.

Setting up interviews

As a routine part of the job, a publicist arranges media interviews for clients/employers. The majority of these will involve artists, and part of the skill is to link each one with the most suitable journalists and offer potential interviewers a mutually appropriate (and sometimes exclusive) angle. On the one hand, popular artists will be in such media demand that some interview requests will have to be turned down. On the other hand, unknown newcomers or rising stars will need the publicist's push. Often the two extremes can be linked when a little subtle leverage is brought into play by the publicist.

Arranging photography

As with writers and broadcasting journalists, photographers fall into two main categories, freelance and staff. Among the freelancers are those who specialize in specific areas such as album sleeve photography. When pictures of an artist are being taken to accompany a particular article, the publicist may have less say in selecting a photographer by name because the decision will belong to the journalist or picture editor. Otherwise, it is up to the publicist to learn which photographers work best with which artists. Good rapport between the two should produce substantially better pictures. Past experience helps the publicist to choose the best freelance photographer for each different situation.

Travelling

The frequency of a publicist's out-of-town trips will vary hugely according to the jobs in hand. A major artist on the road for a large series of concerts may require on-site PR services at each new leg of the tour to handle media interviews and set up press conferences. The publicist should be prepared to travel, often at short notice, sometimes to accompany an important journalist to a gig and occasionally to cope with an unexpected surge of media interest (negative or positive) somewhere on the road.

Receptions and conferences

Media receptions or cocktail parties are held to launch publicity campaigns and are used to introduce new bands/artists, sometimes via a showcase stage performance. Few such events are expected to generate immediate media headlines but are arranged more to create general goodwill and prepare the way for more specific media situations later on. The publicist's role on these occasions is to circulate and make on-the-spot introductions around the room.

Press conferences are more formal and should involve the announcement of some sort of news. Typically they are based on the distribution of a press release and a 'live' question-and-answer session in which the concerned parties face rows of journalists and their photographers from behind a table. As a rule, the publicist acts as moderator, controlling the flow of questioning.

Hand holding and ego massaging

There is no escaping the fact that an element of ego massaging creeps into any situation involving work with performing artists. For example, the publicist must overflow with tact and discretion when asked by the artist to comment on a new record or last night's concert.

The average publicist may also be expected to perform the duties of a social secretary from time to time, securing theatre tickets for top shows when an artist flies in, booking tables at fashionable dining clubs or getting an out-of-town artist into an exclusive nightspot. Officially, these tasks are not part of the publicist's job description, but to an artist they can appear as important as acquiring press exposure!

International PR

Increasingly nowadays music business marketing strategies are scaled up to pancontinental or even global level because the majority of recording and songwriting deals are international and record releases happen simultaneously in many widespread territories. The publicist's role at an international level can range from taking full control of a multi-territory PR campaign to merely coordinating with colleagues and counterparts overseas. At this stage, a knowledge of second and third languages becomes a massive asset.

Most of the above applies to both salaried in-house publicists and freelance independent consultants. The freelance operator has additional factors to consider, including the acquisition, keeping and replacing of clients, the fixing and collection of fees and the actual management of the PR business. Some consultants aim to take on the longest possible roster of clients, serving each on a very superficial level but also charging relatively low monthly or quarterly fees. Others prefer to keep their list short, devoting more time to each one, charging appropriately more and looking for long-term year-round relationships with those they represent rather than handling short 'one-off' campaigns.

Probably the most sensible policy for the beginner is to build up a mix of both types of client and gradually move towards one or other end of the spectrum in the wake of personal experience. It is virtually impossible to discuss fee structures here because the amount a publicist charges must be based on so many varying factors. Most fees are based on time spent, but some publicists simply propose the largest figure they think the client will stand for in the prevailing circumstances. The better the industrial reputation of the publicist, the higher the fees can be pushed. As with any other line of business, the independent publicist risks financial failure if incoming fees do not cover payroll and other overheads.

The nature of the PR business means that most people who enter it hope to have made a career-long choice. On the other hand, it is quite possible to use PR as a stepping stone in the music industry. There are several contemporary record company bosses, men and women, who have risen to boardroom level from positions in the press office.

Indeed, the fact that specific specialist qualifications are not essential means that it is very possible for clerks, typists, telephonists and other general office assistants to make excellent headway in a company press office or any independent PR consultancy solely as a result of displaying the right flair.

THE WAYS INTO THE BUSINESS

There is a range of routes which can lead to a career as a music industry publicist. It is possible to follow one or more of these:

• Academic tuition. At the time of writing, 10 universities and colleges throughout England, Scotland and the Republic of Ireland offer courses in public relations or communication whose degrees and diplomas are recognized by the London-based Institute Of Public Relations for membership purposes. Theoretically such courses provide a sound fundamental knowledge of PR machinery, but not of its practical application within the music business. Students often gain mid-course hands-on experience by offering their (unpaid) services to a suitable company (in this case a record company press office or independent publicist's consultancy) during long vacations.

• Journalistic experience. Working for a local hometown newspaper or broadcaster can be a useful starting point, particularly if the chance exists to review concerts or records. A journalist receives press releases from publicists and learns to separate the useful and informative material from the badly written or badly targeted stuff, a most valuable experience. Would-be publicists unable to get a job on a newspaper or radio station can still submit reviews and other articles on music topics to features editors and programme producers on a freelance basis: whether or not they are published, the writing experience will be worthwhile.

• Experience in the music industry. Juniors in a record company press office can pick up a lot of useful industrial knowledge. Some get the chance to fill in for more senior people from time to time. The would-be publicist learns from what goes on and is not afraid to put forward ideas.

• Experience with an independent publicist. As an alternative to working within a music industry company, the trainee can try for a job as a temporary or part-time PR assistant in a PR consultancy. This may mean making the coffee and faxing out press releases, but it can also lead to more valuable opportunities such as writing artists' biography sheets or phoning through news stories to the trade papers.

Only after accumulating sufficient qualifications by way of academic achievement and/or useful work experience should you contemplate applying for a publicist's job, probably with a record company. The majors tend to look for a postgraduate degree in music management or something similar. Smaller independent companies will take much less in the way of academic achievement if aspects of a candidate's personality seem to be right for the job. Hunt through adverts in the trade papers.

The personnel department will be concerned with what you did at school and/or university, how you fared in English and foreign languages and whether you've been through any courses in public relations. The senior press officer may want to look at anything you've written in the way of concert or record reviews but your personality will also be under particular scrutiny.

At this stage, timidity, uncertainty, hesitation or an inability to put across your own best features will go against you. Moderate self-confidence, self-salesmanship, a controlled sense of humour, some intelligently inquisitive questions about the work you might be doing and a show of interest in the label's artists will go down well. Most important of all, let your interviewer(s) see how much you know about the media in general and about the key publications and columnists with whom you hope to be in working contact.

12

Music and the media

Without the media, the mass-market music business as we know it today would not be able to function. By the *media*, we mean the daily, even hourly, bombardment of images and sounds which we receive from magazines, newspapers, radio, television and video; by the *mass-market music business* we mean the business which releases over 200 rock, pop and dance singles and albums a week in the UK alone.

People who buy pop records usually buy them because they've heard them on the radio, seen the artist or artists in question on television or read about them in a magazine. Many others, of course, buy records because they hear about them through friends, or are exposed to them at clubs or perhaps in the cinema. However, few in the music business would deny that it is the media, particularly radio and the printed word, which gets its message across most effectively and to the largest number of people.

To the lay person, the means by which a record gets played on the radio or gets reviewed in a magazine or newspaper might seem somewhat random. A DJ gives a record a listen, decides he or she likes it and puts it on the list for tomorrow's show. Or a music journalist keeps a look out for the latest album by this band or that singer and once it is released, takes it home, plays it, makes notes and comes into the office the next day to write the review.

It doesn't happen like this.

Record companies are all too aware of the value of radio airplay to leave it to chance. They are also all too aware of the fact that music journalists get bombarded with many thousands of records, year-in, year-out. If a journalist is going to pay special attention to a particular release, the record company is going to have to pay special attention to that journalist.

THE PLUGGER

The smiley, cheery myth that the average radio DJ serves to perpetuate is that his or her station has its finger on the pulse, will always seek out the best in new music for your listening pleasure, and that music radio and music business together enjoy a relationship of mutual backslapping and mutual love of a good tune.

Not true.

If it was true, there would be no need for *pluggers*. All major record companies employ, at great cost, teams of men and women whose sole job is to supply radio stations with records and then to persuade radio producers and DJs to play them.

It's a tough and often soul-destroying job, but one which can bring considerable rewards, in terms of both job satisfaction and hard cash. A plugger with a good track record can be worth millions to a record company and will be rewarded accordingly.

AIRPLAY

Although radio has become less important to the music business than it used to be, even in the nineties it remains the single most effective way of breaking a popular music act, and of selling records in all genres. For not only does radio airplay *expose* a piece of music to hundreds, thousands and in some cases even millions of potential purchasers, it almost always shows that piece of music in a good light. How often do you hear a DJ announce a record by telling you how awful it is? Answer: never! Because if a DJ were to admit to playing bad records, that's tantamount to admitting that the show is a bad show.

Radio stations and DJs provide an extraordinarily good service to the record companies and their artists. They advertise their records by playing them, they tell the audience how wonderful their records are and, they *pay* the songwriter, publisher and artist for the privilege! Hence the importance of airplay to record companies and the reason why they spend fortunes on teams of pluggers.

WHAT THE PLUGGER DOES

There is no one proven method of plugging a record. Each plugger has his or her own style, because in this particular area of the music business it's the end rather than the means that is most important.

First, the record in question must reach producer and/or DJ. A simple task, you might think, except that in many radio stations these people won't open the post, and certainly won't come to the reception to meet a total stranger. Even if the record does eventually end up in their hands, what's to stop them simply placing it in the *to be ignored* pile or even the trash can? So after the simple job of getting the record to the producer/DJ, the plugger's next job is to make sure they *notice* the record and *want to hear it*.

Here's where the ingenuity of the plugger and the support given to the plugger by the record company comes into play. If the marketing, press, promotions and PR people have done their jobs properly, the record in question will have been the subject of an effective marketing campaign and both producer and DJ will be simply dying to hear it. But this rarely happens. Few records will get such priority treatment, and many of those which do will automatically make it to the playlist anyway. Where the pluggers have their work cut out is in cases where the record they are plugging is by unknowns, or by artists whose last record flopped.

In such cases pluggers will try anything. Producers, particularly those at 1FM (formerly BBC Radio 1), tell tales of pluggery which sound like pure fiction: tales of pluggers dressing up as cartoon characters, pluggers dressing up as policemen, pluggers sending records frozen in blocks of ice, pluggers offering expensive gifts, pluggers sending strippergrams, pluggers turning up on horseback, pluggers offering bribes of money, cars, holidays and even drugs in an attempt to get their records noticed.

The above is a list of exceptions rather than a picture of how plugging works on a day-to-day basis. All the above examples have actually happened, but typically pluggers succeed in the long term by building up strong personal relationships with radio stations, their producers and DJs. Again, how this is done depends upon the people concerned, but the tried-and-tested business lunch usually plays an important part here.

Once this relationship is established, the plugger won't have such a hard time getting in to see the producer or DJ when a new record requires exposure. Also, if the relationship is a sound one, and the plugger earns a good reputation among DJs and producers, then much time will be saved when the plugger does have product to push, as he or she will be able to come directly to the point without having to resort to gimmicks to win attention.

THE PLAYLIST

In a large radio station like the BBC's national pop station in the UK, 1FM, it is the producer who has the greatest say over what gets played, and will fashion the playlist of his or her particular show according to the presenter's style and the *house playlist* – the list of records that can and can't be played for various reasons which is decided upon weekly at a meeting. So in such a case it is the producers who are targeted by the pluggers. In the UK, in spite of the increase in the number of radio stations, most pluggers will agree that 1FM airplay is their ultimate goal for any popular record.

The computerized playlist

On all but a very few stations (1FM being an exception) radio playlists (the schedule of titles which are today played across the station's output in any given week) are put together by off-the-shelf computer programs. New titles with accompanying identifying information are fed into the computer on a weekly basis, and the computer then works out what should be played and when. So in such cases even the individual programme producer won't necessarily have any say over what records are included in the programme. The plugger will therefore have to find out who at the station has the job of programming the computer on a weekly basis. In small local radio stations this might be a senior executive, perhaps the programme controller, or someone blessed with the title head of music or music producer.

Television

Although pluggers tend to concentrate their efforts on radio, there is also value in television and club exposure. In television, certainly in the UK and Europe, there are few opportunities to push a new record. If breakfast television, children's weekend shows or daytime magazine programmes have slots, they will always be filled where possible by a newsworthy name, and one which suits the target audience. Television appearances always do serve as helpful promotion but, unlike radio airplay, they will never (or rarely) be repeated. While it might be worthwhile spending up to 2 months to persuade a radio station to play one single – because if it gets on the playlist it's likely to be played and played and may even become a hit – to put the same effort into a 3-minute television appearance which might be pulled at the last minute can be considerably less productive.

Television appearances will not be as straightforward as radio airplay. In many cases television programme producers and researchers will seek out particular acts because they are currently *hot* or visually impressive. Likewise, they may reject a particular act because it doesn't work visually. The best chance any act will have of getting on television (apart from a performance slot on a live specialist music programme) will be as part of a marketing push that will include a single and/or an album with accompanying video and a tour. Such a situation would make an act highly interviewable on the typical daytime television sofa, because there would be tour dates and a record to talk about as well as a video clip to show. Such an appearance would, however, not always be left to the plugger to coordinate; the record company promotions department and the act's management is very likely to be involved here.

Then, of course, there's MTV, which, apart from its increasing number of specialist programmes, operates rather like a visual radio station. To get a video *in rotation* on MTV will always be the goal of any record company, although MTV's playlist is even more restrictive than those of most radio stations. Your video must have *the MTV look*, whatever that is at any given time, and will stand little chance if the artist in question is not known.

The clubs

Pluggers working for an indie, a dance label particularly, will ignore the clubs at their peril. In the nineties, as radio stations have become more rigid in their music programming, and as many of the new radio stations play no new records at all (the so-called gold stations), so young people are going elsewhere to enjoy music together. The rave phenomenon of the late eighties/early nineties has spawned a whole new type of act – and sector of the business – which gets little mass-media attention, which puts out records on tiny indie labels (Chapter 3) and which can make a fair amount of money doing so.

A rave or rave-style gathering, after all, can bring literally thousands of people together in one place. If you can convince the club DJ there that your record will suit the occasion, it will subsequently enjoy a large, captive audience. If it proves popular it will be requested again and again, and subsequently be bought by a number of the clubbers present.

Clubs also provide a useful means of exposure for small indies which simply can't afford pluggers. Mailing out a few hundred records to key club DJs is a relatively cheap way of getting exposure for a record. If the DJs get a good response from the record, they will not only play it frequently but they will want to know if there's more where that came from. Club DJs are also a rich source of information for A&R people, management companies and any other sector of the music business on the look out for tried-and-tested new talent.

International

Radio airplay doesn't have the same impact wherever you are in the world. The UK's situation is quite unique in that pop radio has been dominated by Radio 1 (now 1FM) since 1970. In the US, on the other hand, the radio audience is divided – geographically, by time zones and by musical genre. An act that can make it big in one state might never do the same in another; an act which is enjoying *heavy rotation* on one little local FM station might not be being played anywhere else in the country.

In parts of Europe there are quotas which restrict the number of *foreign* records that can be played on the air, and in many other parts of the world there are places where no foreign acts get heard on the radio at all.

So for an international release, local plugging task forces or the equivalent are required, and the local licensor or the local branch of the international record company will coordinate this. Pluggers working in more than one territory are therefore a rarity.

BECOMING A PLUGGER

Good pluggers make good money. Not all record companies can afford to employ full-time pluggers so many work freelance and go on to form plugging companies (usually called promotions companies), some employing 15 or more people. Such companies often then apply their talents and list of contacts to other work such as PR and even management.

To become a plugger won't necessarily require any specific formal qualifications, but here are a few qualifications which most promotions companies will look out for in potential employees:

- Sales experience. Plugging or promoting a record is basically a selling job. Sales training or sales experience will help you into a plugging or *promotions* company.

- A good knowledge of the media, radio in particular, and a good knowledge of music will be crucial if you're to prove to a potential employer that you can keep on top of this fast-moving business.

- Personability. Meeting with producers and DJs is a sociable job. Confidence and a pleasant manner will be essential here. You must also be presentable and have good communication skills. Basics such as a clean driving licence will also help.

Most of all, however, you will have to have boundless energy, a thick skin and the will and desire to succeed in a tough business. And the rewards can be considerable. An independent plugger will be able to claim a share in the profits in a particular record at the time of drawing up the contract with record company and/or artists' management; a plugger employed by a record company who proves valuable to the company will, up to a point, be able to state his or her price – and if the record company won't pay that price, there'll be other record companies or independent plugging companies that will.

Also, interestingly enough, many pluggers go on to high-profile jobs within the business or the media – as radio or television producers or even presenters or even into record company management. Successful pluggers have, after all, proved that they can get what they want often against considerable odds, while remaining liked, or at least respected, by people within the industry – and that's not an easy thing to achieve.

THE DISC JOCKEY

Radio DJ wanted. Fun working conditions, lots of free records, good pay, meet the stars. Send your CV to ...

How often do you see a job like that advertised? Never is the answer. Look at the job description and you'll see why. The radio DJ's job is a wonderful job. Few will ever tell you otherwise. They get to play (and to keep) all the best, or at least the most popular, of the latest record releases; they often get to meet the people who appear on the records; they're wooed and flattered by record companies; they can become celebrities, which in turn gives them a further means of making money; *and* they get paid for all this!

Of course it's not quite as straightforward as that. This is a highly competitive area of work. There are few music stations in the UK: two national pop stations (1FM and Virgin 1215 on AM), two classical stations (Radio Three and Classic FM) and a jazz station (J-FM, which can be heard in London and the northwest). Most of the remaining stations which play music across the UK are community stations (often aimed at ethnic or other minorities) or BBC and independent local radio (ILR) stations. Local radio stations are restricted in the amount of music they play, partly because it costs money and partly because the terms of their licences state that they must include an element of public service broadcasting, be they independent or a part of the BBC.

Getting the job

The job of DJ being a rare one therefore, how do you set about getting that job? Answer: you push yourself. The aspiring music radio DJ will have set up a mobile disco at as young an age as possible. With this equipment he or she will get *gigs* at local discos, weddings and so on. This will earn the aspiring DJ both money and experience. The DJ will become well known, while keeping in regular touch with a local radio station or two. Eventually a vacancy will become free at one of these stations and a DJ who has done a good enough PR job may stand a chance of getting it.

Alternatively, you will have got yourself a job (unpaid) at your nearest hospital radio station. Here you will develop a style, and have the luxury of being able to prepare a tape of your best moments on radio, which you will have duplicated and sent around to every radio station in the country, or at least every radio station you might want to work for.

You may, on the other hand, want to gain your pre-radio experience as a club DJ. This you will only be able to do:

- by making such a good name for yourself doing weddings and so on that you're asked to DJ at the local club;

- by proving, in whatever way, to the club manager that you're right for the place;

- by starting your own club.

As a club DJ you will begin to serve as a useful indicator to your record suppliers (specialist shops, record companies, etc.) of what the club audience is listening to. In such a specialist role you will stand a better chance of getting on-air work once it becomes available as your name will become known in certain circles which matter.

And yes, the getting of a straight music radio DJ's job is as haphazard as that. When you think about it, it always has been. The early DJs were, mainly, pirates (those who were brave enough to risk making illegal broadcasts in order to provide the UK with non-stop music radio, unavailable until 1969 when Radio 1 was launched). Some of these are *still* broadcasting now! The newcomers to national radio are being selected from different walks of life: journalism, television, stand-up comedy. There's no law about what makes a good DJ and there is no law about why station bosses choose particular people for the job.

It's tough now, certainly at national level, to get radio DJ work unless you're already famous for something else.

Anything else, some may say, other than being a radio DJ!
There is always something to be said for working your way up
through the small local radio stations (which pay very badly),
however. Because even in this increasingly competitive area of
the business, talent does occasionally win through.

THE MUSIC PRESS

The way in which the music press, and the press generally, is
made aware of a particular artist or band is explained in
Chapter 11. Both the press offices of record companies and independent press and PR companies will have to be fully aware of
who's writing for what magazine or newspaper, what the circulation and the reader profile of those publications are and when
an announcement should be made in order to exploit as many
publications as possible. What this means for the music journalist is that he or she will never have to look far for a story. This
also means, however, that the music journalist is likely to have
to look a little further for a really strong story, one which the
record company press offices or PRs haven't engineered and
one that all the other music papers and magazines haven't got.

THE PUBLICATIONS

The music press in the UK can be divided broadly into three
sections:

- music trade papers;
- weekly consumer music papers ;
- monthly consumer music magazines.

The trade press

These papers or magazines exist to serve the music business
itself. They are staffed by expert journalists who keep in constant touch with all aspects of the music business, and who put
together stories, features and reports which serve to inform
everyone in the music business of what their colleagues and
rivals are up to.

The leading trade title in the UK is *Music Week*. You will find the latest copy of this magazine on the desk of every self-respecting record company executive in the land. As well as keeping the industry informed about takeovers, mergers, promotions and demotions in the business, it advises retailers about press and advertising campaigns for particular releases, informs them in advance of music coverage on radio and television, publishes a weekly release list of singles and albums and the national singles and album charts. *Music Week* also offers in-depth stories on any change in government policy which might affect the music business as well as following changes in copyright laws and developments in the fight against piracy and keeping in close touch with the various music business trade bodies.

Other music trade publications which are important to people working in the UK music business include *Billboard*, which looks at the international music business, although heavily US biased; *Music and Media*, which looks at the Europe-wide industry; and the glossy monthly *Music Business International*.

Such trade magazines have to be strong on factual information and much of the writing trade journalists are required to do is therefore more objective than subjective. Journalists working at this end of the music press spectrum tend to meet and interview the executives rather than the stars and may well travel the globe, but to attend overseas music business fairs rather than to follow a superstar on tour. One common factor between the trade journalist and the consumer journalist (see below) is the *freebie* – the industry term for the free gift. Work on the music side of radio, television, trade or consumer press and you will never have to buy a record again, or a t-shirt for that matter, as long as you don't mind your t-shirts covered with logos and slogans.

The consumer music papers

In this context, consumer means the record-buying public. A wide range of papers and magazines are published weekly and monthly to satisfy the avid rock and pop fan. Statistics show that the readerships of these publications are lower than in the heyday of the sixties and seventies, but most of the leading titles of today are well established: the weekly music paper *Melody Maker*, for example, was established just after the Second World War.

The weeklies

These look like tabloid newspapers, are usually very thick and aim to cover the mainstream acts fully as well as to be ahead of current trends by *discovering* the next fashionable act.

The best-established of these weeklies are the *New Musical Express* (*NME*) and the *Melody Maker*. The former has the reputation of being the more *left field* of the two (although *Melody Maker* regularly holds its own with the *NME* in terms of keeping one step ahead of what's new and *happening*), while *Melody Maker* tends to give heavy rock music more column space than the *NME*.

Broadly speaking there's little between them. Many rock and pop fans will take both, otherwise it's all down to a matter of taste.

What these weeklies do for the music business is provide exposure for new, upcoming and established artists. These publications are, however, entirely independent from the music business, and therefore are as free to destroy an artist's credibility as they are to build it up.

All the music papers, like all newspapers, will claim that their editorial is never affected by outside pressure. However, it is clear that there are trade-offs. One favourite trick by PRs and press officers is to offer a big-name artist for a feature (complete with flights to the live show in New York for the journalist), as long as the paper also gives column space to this or that newcomer. There are other tricks of the trade, on both sides, but by and large the impression given to the reader is that the weeklies have a strong independent voice and will say if they don't like a record or an artist or both.

The monthlies

The monthly magazines, meanwhile, take a longer, more lingering look at the artists, the records and the music scene generally. The leading titles in the UK are *Vox*, *Q* and *MoJo*, the last two being aimed at the older 18–35(+) readership, while *Vox* is pitched at a similar audience to that of the *NME* or *Melody Maker*: the 13–24 age group. The US publication *Rolling Stone*, also published in the UK, is pitched at the *Q/MoJo* audience.

These monthlies are colourful, less newsy (they work 4–6

weeks ahead of publication date while the papers can work on stories up until a couple of days before going to print) and tend to reflect rather than set trends. Their style tends to be more ponderous, the writing more deliberately entertaining, and they serve to provide the background to the current scene rather than aiming to be a part of it, as the weeklies might claim to be.

To be a journalist on a music trade paper, a weekly music paper or one of the monthly glossies is regarded as particularly special. The jobs are few and far between, they offer considerable perks (free records, foreign travel, parties) and despite long, stressful hours can bring immense satisfaction. On the downside, the pay's not great, at least until you become a reasonably established name.

The specialist publications

There are specialist publications in all areas of the music press. Specialist trade publications include *Applause*, which is aimed at the live performance side of the business and will therefore be of interest to anyone from venue owners and managers to equipment hire companies. Specialist consumer titles include *Kerrang!*, which focuses on heavy metal and hard rock acts, *Blues & Soul Magazine* and *Folk Roots*.

THE MUSIC JOURNALIST'S JOB

There are variations between the type of work carried out by the journalists working in the three different types of publication mentioned above. A typical day on a trade paper might involve collecting and collating industry data, while on a weekly consumer title a typical day might involve sifting through press releases, which will then have to be followed up by phone calls, in order to put together a column of short news stories for one of the news pages in the paper. On a glossy monthly, a typical day might involve going out to a recording studio somewhere, with a photographer, to interview an artist or band in the wake of a new album release. If the journalist concerned is lucky that studio might be in New York or the Caribbean, in which case the trip might take up to a week. If the journalist is unlucky, the studio will be in the middle of a choked-up city in the UK and the day will be wet and cold. The piece the journalist has to write subsequent to this visit must be fresh, lively and entertaining, despite the chosen venue.

Journalists on all these three types of publication will experience a mixture of routine and more glamorous jobs. The trade papers offer the opportunity for journalists to travel the world to trade fairs and occasionally to interview key figures in the business; the weeklies follow the stars around the world, review concerts and events as well as records, books and videos, while the monthlies have their own fair share of routine work – compiling news and reviews pages and other information-heavy sections of the publication.

BECOMING A MUSIC JOURNALIST

Jobs in music journalism don't come easy, because so many people want to work in this field. On the rare occasion that such a job is advertised – either a staff writer, editorial assistant or similar – the personnel department of the company concerned will always receive hundreds and even thousands of applications. So you have to be special, or you have to get noticed somehow. There are no strict rules about getting into music journalism; some publications will insist on an NCTJ qualification (National Council for the Training of Journalists – see Appendix B) and that will always be useful to have whether or not the publications you're interested in working for insist on it. An NCTJ qualification plus one of the music business qualifications listed at the back would serve you very well in your aim to become a music journalist.

On the other hand, many music journalists learned the hard way, by starting their own fanzines (Chapter 15) or simply by bothering the music papers with phone calls, visits and unsolicited reviews, interviews and stories until someone stood up and took notice of them.

If you do keep sending in your articles and reviews, and if they are any good, and if you can suffer the indignity of not even having them acknowledged for months and even a year or more, then the chances are that you'll get somewhere in the end.

The way to get into music journalism is to practise your craft (get others to read your work and *accept criticism!*), send it out to as many editors as you can, get out to concerts and put your face about how and wherever you can, until someone takes notice.

If you do go down this extrovert, *pushy* route, you must also make sure that you come across as reasonably likeable and not too overbearing. Newsrooms are busy, pressured places to work and any member of staff's personability is going to count as much as if not more than pure talent.

FREELANCE

In many cases, if your unsolicited reviews or articles are accepted by a publication, that might be as far as it goes. The editor (or section editor, news editor, reviews editor, live concert editor, etc.) might accept the piece, instruct the accounts department to pay you for it – at a standard rate per line, per column inch or per word – publish it and that is that: no job offer at the end of it all.

What you will hopefully get is a *byline* or name credit, which means you can then use this piece of published work to get other work. Build up relationships in this way with a number of editors, each of whom pays you for work used, and suddenly you can call yourself a freelance journalist. More and more music and other journalists are working in this way as publications cut down on permanent staff. It's scary, because often you don't know where the next piece of work is coming from. On the other hand, you choose your pace of work and your employers. And if you're good, they'll always choose you.

13

The concert promoter

Think for a minute about what's involved in the staging of even an average-sized rock concert. A venue has to be booked; payment for that venue has to be guaranteed; a contract for the booking of that venue has to be drawn up and signed; the band concerned has to be certain that the facilities exist for all its equipment and stage set; equipment that isn't owned by the band has to be hired; there must be vehicle access to get the equipment in; there has to be somewhere for those vehicles to park until the end of the concert; there has to be back stage and front-of-house security; there have to be changing and hospitality facilities; there has to be an audience so there has to be promotion; tickets have to be sold, and at the right price; and if the tickets don't get sold, staff and concert hall owner have to be paid anyway.

All the above are often, ultimately, the sole responsibility of the concert promoter. On top of all this the concert promoter has to run his or her own company too, paying staff, office rental, phone bills, etc.

THE PROMOTER'S JOB

A promoter will not always get involved in all of the above. The job varies from concert to concert, from tour to tour, depending on the type of act, and the type of deal that has been struck between the promoter and that act.

In some cases a promoter will design the set, put the road

crew together, decide how, where and when the performance or performances will take place, book hotels and deal with the real minutiae, such as what sort of fruit will be in the bowl on the table of the lead singer's hotel suite on arrival. In a hands-off deal, on the other hand, the promoter's job might begin and end with the booking of one or a series of venues and dates, with the rest of the work being done by the record company and/or the artist's management.

Taking the example of a major band, working on a big-budget album for which a big-budget marketing campaign is to be planned, here's how the promoter might fit into the scheme of things.

It has been decided by record company and band management that the album should be promoted by a world tour. The band concerned has a tried-and-tested track record as a live act, and there is little doubt that most venues, wherever they are, will sell well. (No promoter would ever assume this, of course, as fashions change fast in the music business, and such an assumption would also devalue the promoter's role.) Such a tour is just the sort of prestige, high-earning enterprise a promoter would be keen to *buy*. And that's exactly how it happens. Band and promoter will come together and, after the scale and logistics of the tour have been clarified, the promoter will make a bid. Let's say the promoter offers £5 million to stage a 100-date world tour for a top-name act. If all are agreed, the promoter will agree to pay that figure to the band, through its management, in return for the 'gate money' earned on the tour. In other words, that £5 million bid, which will cover tour costs and artists' fees, is based on how much the promoter calculates can be earned through ticket sales. The difference between the cost of staging the tour and money *taken on the gate* represents profit or loss to the promoter. It's a high-risk business, but one in which there are fortunes to be made, for all concerned, if all goes to plan.

The deal

It's in the making of the deal that much of a promoter's skill and experience comes into play. How does the promoter know what price to offer? If too much is offered, the promoter stands to lose money, while if too little is offered the promoter stands to lose the tour to another promoter.

Much checking of venue details (the venue will often be arranged through a booking agent, who in turn will take a fee) must be done before too many promises are made by promoter to artist. The promoter must find out when and for how long daytime sound checks can be made; whether the agent will include clauses stating, for example, that the band cannot play within a certain radius of that venue on the same tour; how long a show can last at said venue, and therefore how long a set the support act (if there is one) will be able to perform; whether the venue has its own security; whether there are any local bye-laws which will restrict access for equipment transport; and whether or not there is a maximum ticket price allowable.

Careful study of the market for the act in question and the logistics of the proposed tour will be required, too, before a deal is struck, but even thorough research won't guarantee to the promoter that the final bid is failsafe. An entrepreneurial spirit coupled with plenty of experience (which will reduce the amount of research needed, for example) are the extra factors required to ensure that the bid is the right bid.

Artists' riders

The list of requirements, or *riders*, written into the contract by the artist can often read like a joke to the uninitiated. The example of the right fruit in the fruit bowl is far from extreme in comparison with other riders promoters have had to deal with in tour contracts. A certain type of beer or wine at a certain temperature available back stage at all times; an after-gig masseur; specified amounts of daily cash expenses; a particular type of shampoo in the hotel bathroom; a double bed in the concert hall changing room; a grand piano in the hotel suite. These are not uncommon or unlikely demands. Experienced concert promoters will tell of even more bizarre demands made in the riders on an artists' contract. It is the job of a good promoter either to curb certain excesses if they are going to get in the way of the smooth running or the tour and/or to make sure that the cost of these riders is covered in the contract.

Preparation

A good promoter will work with an act well in advance of the start of a tour, making sure that studio time (if an album is in the making) doesn't overspill into the tour schedule for example. How many times have you heard the phrase 'cancelled due to recording commitments'? This well-used excuse can simply mean that recording went on way past deadline and the album's not ready in time for the tour. (It can also mean that the tour hasn't sold enough tickets, although few will admit this.) The promoter will also work with the band on the live sound, participating in rehearsals and advising what works in certain venues, particularly those venues with which the act is unfamiliar.

The support act

Many support acts buy their way on to tours. The value of a ready-made audience, the accompanying publicity and the kudos attached to supporting certain headline acts make this a worthwhile expenditure (often put up by a record company if the band in question has a contract, or a publisher with which the support act has a deal, or indeed an A&R person who has an interest in signing the support act). The majority of the audience will have paid to see the headline act only, and some are likely to remain in the bar until the support act has left the stage.

The inclusion of the support act is therefore another consideration for the promoter. If it buys on to the tour it will expect certain things in return, such as soundcheck time (Chapter 19), which is something that will have to be negotiated with venue, agent and headliners.

Publicity

In liaison with the record company marketing department (Chapter 9) the promoter will also want to arrange publicity for the tour. Posters at venues and in public areas close to the venues will need to be produced and positioned (legally or illegally); local paper and radio advertising will need to be planned and all such activity will need to be stepped up nearer the concert date, particularly if tickets aren't selling well.

Depending upon the scale of the tour and the allocated budget, this job might be done by a separate company contracted especially to coordinate publicity for the whole tour. For a low-budget tour, a promoter might simply rely on free advertising from a media campaign and poster support close to concert venues only.

Insurance

The list of unpredictable occurrences that can prevent a concert or whole tour from going ahead is endless; some of the items on that list can be insured against, and some cannot. Cancellation because of accident, illness, flood or fire is an insurable hazard; overspending as a result of bad planning or low ticket sales because of lack of popularity of the act in question is not!

A promoter should make certain that the risk of a band splitting up or failing in some other way to keep its side of the deal is covered in the contract. The best insurance against any failure which is not an act of God, however, is experience. A promoter who has been successful in the business for some years will be able to smell a disaster well in advance, and will have a catalogue of damage limitation measures to apply.

The rest of the world

A world tour will, of course, involve staff being employed and bookings being made for shows in other countries. Some (though few) promoters will handle the whole tour from the base country, although most will effectively subcontract the tour to various foreign promoters, each of whom will set up and run a specific *leg* of the tour. This will of course be coordinated by the base promoter in collaboration with the artist and artist's management.

One-off shows

Promoters will not always be working on tours; one-off concerts can be just as profitable, less fraught, easier to plan and usually less risky. If an act wishes to play a one-off for whatever reason, the management will usually first contact one or a series of possible venues through booking agents. The agent for the chosen venue will then contact a number of promoters, each of whom will put in a bid for the show. The agent will usually go for the highest bid (more cash for the agent), and then a contract will be drawn up between promoter, agent and management.

As with the tour, in such a one-off situation, the promoter will pay a lump sum for the privilege of promoting the gig, and this sum will finance the whole venture in the hope that income earned from ticket sales will cover costs and leave a reasonable profit at the end.

Promoters are increasingly becoming proactive in the business and, rather than waiting to be approached by band, manager or agent, will create a show from concept to final execution. Such shows usually need to be more than just a gig: they have to be *events* in order that an audience can be persuaded to attend whether or not they are fans of the actual performers. So a massive, open-air performance of a popular opera might be staged, or a number of artists who would not normally appear on the same bill might be brought together, the novelty value of the event being the attraction rather than just the artists themselves. Such one-offs can be most lucrative, especially if the *television rights* can be sold.

Sponsorship

Today's large-scale tours require large-scale budgets, and if some of this money can be recouped through a sponsorship deal few artists will these days refuse to allow a particular brand name to ally itself with their success.

So soft drink brand names, credit card company logos and other familiar images adorn an increasing number of concert posters and tickets, venue entrances and sometimes even stage space, in return for often large sums of money which go to cover artists' fees and tour costs, and which can often serve to reduce the promoter's risk at the same time.

BECOMING A PROMOTER

Tempted? The financial rewards can be considerable, and the job satisfaction immense, if all goes well that is. The coming together of performer and audience is always a unique event, and when that teaming really works the experience can be described as not far short of religious for both parties. As promoter, to be the catalyst which sparked this spiritual moment must be truly satisfying. Oh yes, and there's the money too.

Promoters can make fortunes; they can lose fortunes too, but those who do either manage to cover their losses on the next tour or pull out altogether. Strangely, there are promoters operating in the business today who, over the years, have been close to bankruptcy on many occasions and yet still carry on. In such cases it's either that they're making undisclosed sums of money which keep them going (there are many ways this can be done in the concert promotion business, think of all those cash payments made for tickets, and who's counting the number of people going in?) or they're in it for the love or the thrill of the business. Either way, it's the chosen profession of many, and yet another of those music business jobs where personality, experience and attitude count as much as, if not more than, qualifications.

Many concert promoters started out by booking bands for college dances and concerts, the UK's best-known promoter, Harvey Goldsmith, being one such example. This is one excellent, low-risk means by which to learn the promoter's trade. Artist management is another way of learning the promoter's trade as, often in the early days of an artist's career, managers will do the work of a promoter themselves.

To join a concert promotion company you might need anything from a good telephone manner (for a job as one of the people who deals with ticket availability enquiries and so on) to artist management experience (if you're to be dealing with managers yourself) or even legal qualifications if the promotion company is of the size at which it can afford to employ its own lawyers.

Experience of the workings of concert venues as a booking agent or front-of-house manager perhaps could be valuable if you were considering a move into concert promotion; work as an artist's tour manager, too, would provide valuable experience.

DOING THE JOB

The concert promoter is one of the people at the sharp end of the music business. He or she does meet the stars, does go to the shows and does fly around the world to check out venues, meet managers and artists and even local VIPs if the concert in question is to be a big event. That's at the high-risk, high-earning end of the business. At the other end is the man or woman who spends most of a working week on the phone striking deals with local venue managers, *flyposter* gangs, local noise abatement people, police and councillors all for the sake of a reasonably well-known act which is playing a one-off gig at the local theatre.

There are jobs in a typical working week which are common to both the high flyer and the locally based desk-bound concert promoter, and they include:

- employing, dealing with and paying a lawyer to oversee agreements with venue manager, artist's management and bank;

- ensuring that all necessary insurances are in place – from personal liability insurance against anything going wrong on the night to insurance against cancellation of the performance for whatever reason;

- raising the finance and/or securing credit to pay for the staging of a show or tour before any income has been received from ticket sales;

- advertising the show to ensure maximum ticket sales.

- meeting artists' managers and checking out new acts with a view to securing and developing future business;

- lobbying venue owners, venue managers and booking agents over the general improvement of terms and conditions;

- generally keeping pace with what's popular in the particular market in which the promoter operates.

It can all sound rather dull and routine when listed in this way; in fact it is never either. Although it may be frustrating, stressful and nerve-wracking, the job of the concert promoter is never dull or routine because the concert promoter always has two important unknowns upon which success depends: the performance and the audience. If the performance isn't up to scratch, and the audience isn't as big as was hoped for, then income, reputations and future business suffers. If, on the other hand, both live up to expectations, then there's money to be made, which, in turn, can be invested in the future. Concert promotion is a high-risk business, but few who are involved would deny that it's also a highly invigorating and even enjoyable one.

Business acumen

A love of music of course helps in concert promotion, but without a shrewd business brain that love could be your ruin. Too many people have suffered financially through their attempts to promote an act purely because they love what that act does. It is important that the concert promoter leaves the art to the artist and is able to step back and look at the financial viability of that act. Take all the advice you need from *those in the artistic know* but base your final decision on whether or not, in the cold light of day, your calculations and your business brain tell you that this act on this tour will make enough at least to cover costs.

14

The merchandisers

We have all, at some time or another, fallen prey to the rock and roll merchandiser. Most times at most gigs we don't buy the t-shirt, the concert programme, the scarf or the baseball hat. But everyone has at least one band or singer that means so much to them that, just that once, as a memento of a once-in-a-lifetime experience, they will splash out over and above the cost of the ticket for something they can take home and keep.

String a whole load of those once-in-a-lifetime experiences together, week after week, month after month, year after year, and you've got a merchandising industry. We can certainly talk today of an industry, for a small but very sophisticated one now exists. Go back just a decade or two, however, and the story is very different. Our starting point frequently in this book has been the moment The Beatles signed to EMI, yet in the case of the merchandising business the starting point comes much later. Merchandising is one area where the Fab Four and their otherwise ground-breaking management machine failed.

Anyone who was around during the Beatlemania years will remember the rush to buy anything Beatles – moptop wigs, John Lennon caps and glasses, Beatle dolls – anything to give people the feeling that they had a piece of the Fab Four. There was so much Beatles merchandise around, in fact, that much of it is still available today and is catalogued in a book called *Beatles for Sale: The Beatles Memorabilia Guide* (published by Virgin). What will surprise many, however, is that John, Paul, George, Ringo, EMI Records and even their manager, the late Brian Epstein, made little or no money from the sale of this merchandise. It has been said that, before The Beatles, the only similarly merchandisable phenomenon had been the characters created by Walt Disney. There was, therefore, no existing framework with which The Beatles could easily exploit their marketability. Thus, much of the money to be made from Beatles merchandise fell into the hands of the forward-thinking Americans who, back in the early sixties at least, were light years ahead of the British in most things commercial.

While the Americans were proving expert at exploiting The Beatles' talents through selling t-shirts, posters, caps and dolls in their image, what they really wanted were some Beatles of their own. And so they created The Monkees, representing perhaps the most successful piece of merchandising in the history of rock and roll. For The Monkees were entirely fabricated from nothing. American writer/director/producer Bob Rafelson teamed with entrepreneur Bert Schneider back in 1965 to form the Raybeat company with the sole purpose of producing a sitcom based on The Beatles' movie *A Hard Day's Night*. The final cast of four was recruited from 437 hopefuls (among which were Monkees rejects Charles Manson and Stephen Stills). Top producers and directors were brought in to create the perfect series, which was launched in the autumn of 1966, and the cream of America's songwriting talent, notably Gerry Goffin, Carole King, Neil Sedaka and Neil Diamond, worked on the repertoire.

Many said it wouldn't work, yet for a while the ensuing Monkeemania looked little different from the Beatlemania which had happened a couple of years earlier. Records sold in their millions and, ironically, so did the spin-off merchandise, created in the image of a band which to start with was little more than a piece of merchandise itself.

The two examples here serve to illustrate a simple point: on the merchandising side of the rock and roll business there is much money to be made, but it won't come to you automatically – you have to work at it.

THE PERFECT COTTAGE INDUSTRY

Rather like the *bedroom indie* described in Chapter 3, it is possible to start your own merchandising concern with very little outlay. If you were to approach a big-name act – U2, Bobby

Brown or REM for example – offering to run their merchandising for them, they'd want an advance of millions for the privilege. And that's basically how it works in the big time: the merchandiser advances a pre-agreed sum to the act in question (or more likely to the manager of the act in question) and then takes control of the whole operation. Like the promoter who 'buys' a tour from a band (Chapter 13), the merchandiser working in this way has to get the sums right from the start, ensuring that the money paid to the artist or management at least equals, or is less than, the money that will be earned from the sale of the merchandise, for in this difference lies the merchandiser's profit.

For the beginner, what's recommended is that you attach yourself to a particular act, let's say a band, and perhaps one of which you are a fan or one which regularly attracts a large and loyal local following. Get to know how this band works live, how often the band performs, what the fans are like and try to determine whether or not the band has any kind of future during which a small merchandising business can be built up. Then approach the band, or the manager if there is one. This band would, ideally, not yet have any firm merchandising arrangements in place.

MAKING THE PITCH

So, you know the band and are familiar with its following, and from this knowledge you will have rehearsed your 'pitch'. You suggest to the members and management that they might like a t-shirt designed bearing their logo, which can be sold at their gigs. You might even have some sketches with you as you make your pitch – done either by you or as a favour by a designer who hopes to get the work if you strike the deal (avoid spending money at this stage if possible). If the band has made any demo tapes you might suggest that they consider having a presentation cassette made, which could also be sold at gigs; and if they haven't done any demos, maybe they should. If the band's following is big enough, cassette sales might eventually fund the recording and even end up making the band a small profit.

You will discuss designers (particularly if they don't have a logo and any design ideas themselves) and you will put it to this band that you will organize the design and printing of the t-shirts, stickers, baseball caps and anything else the members might want to offer fans, and will organize the sale of this merchandise at their gigs. If you can, you will finance the whole operation (if you do it little by little the outlay won't be too great) and pay your costs from the profits.

For their part, the band will want to negotiate for a percentage of your profits, and here's where you have to be careful. If they ask for 30% (which would not be unreasonable), you must be clear as to whether that's 30% of your takings or 30% of your profits after costs, tax and VAT have been paid. The two figures will be considerably different. As far as you're concerned, if you believe this band will be a success (and who can ever tell?) then you'll want this deal to run and run. The person who stuck at it, selling 25 t-shirts a night for a year, earning very little money in the process will, after all, want to reap any benefits once that figure grows from 25 to 2500. The trouble is that once the band members see the takings from sales of 2500 t-shirts (which could be approaching £40 000) they're likely to want to increase their share of the action. It's this future scenario that the cottage-industry merchandiser will want to think about right from the start.

THE DEAL

Merchandising deals are almost always struck between management and merchandiser (or band representative and manager if there is no management) rather than between merchandiser and record company. Income from merchandising represents a sum over and above that paid (or lent) to a band from a record company and can often help to subsidize particular projects the record company might not fully support, or might simply serve as extra earnings. Also, there will always be merchandisable bands who don't have record deals.

Record companies might try with young, inexperienced bands to include merchandising in the contract, in other words buy out all or part of the band's merchandising rights. Most managers will advise bands against signing such a deal. There are also record companies with their own merchandising wings, and bands run the risk of losing merchandising rights when signing to such companies.

Most deals will have the act taking 30% of the merchandiser's gross takings. Bearing in mind that in many cases the venue will be taking 25% (see below) and the tax and VAT people their cut, you begin to see why t-shirts at concerts cost so much. That said, if you win the deal to merchandise a world tour by a major international act, there is still much money to be made.

THE CONCERT MERCHANIDISERS' ASSOCIATION

The establishment in the early nineties of the Concert Merchandisers' Association (CMA) in the UK was essentially in response to the UK venues wising up to the profits that were to be made in this area of the music business. At the same time, the forming of the association was a sure sign that the merchandising industry had come of age.

What motivated traditionally rival merchandising companies to establish the association was the announcement by the country's best-known venue, Wembley Stadium, that it was going to put up its commission. Today, all the big venues charge a facility fee: they provide the points of sale and sales staff for official band merchandise and all the merchandiser has to do is provide the goods prior to the opening of the venue on the night.

Merchandisers can no longer set up their own stands and bring in their own staff, which keeps their overheads down but reduces their control over retail, and for this privilege the venues charge 25% of takings.

Just prior to the establishment of the CMA, Wembley decided that it was to raise its fee from 25% to 30%. This decision was influenced by the American management that was running Wembley at the time, for in the US the venue's commission can be anything up to 45%, partly because the US tax system is different. The CMA was formed, initially, to stop this happening, and particularly to prevent other venues from following suit. The merchandisers' united front, which included the suggestion of a merchandising boycott of the venue, persuaded Wembley to keep its commission at 25%.

The CMA members today meet occasionally to discuss new problems and possible solutions, and to keep each other informed of changes and developments in the industry which might affect some or all members. Piracy, for example, is a subject that comes up regularly at CMA gatherings.

PIRACY

The most common complaint among rock and roll merchandisers can be summed up by this remark from a key figure in the
industry: 'If someone copies Walt Disney or Chanel, the police
seem to take action. But if somebody copies Iron Maiden, you're
on your own'.

The law in the UK does little for the merchandiser who falls a
victim to piracy. If someone is caught forging concert tickets, the
police will act. If it is found, however, that someone has printed
an unofficial programme for a particular concert and is selling it
on the streets, the most the police are likely to do is move the
person in question on for causing an obstruction. The pirating of
photographs and artwork for posters, t-shirts or programmes is
a civil offence in the UK, which means that the plaintiff – in this
case the band management, the merchandiser or both – must
take civil action alone, which is costly.

As for what can be registered or copyrighted and what can't,
much of that depends upon the nature of the name of your act.
So big-name bands have spent fortunes getting their names and
logos protected under law, but others will always have problems. Call your band Def Leppard (note the odd spellings) and
you stand a good chance of winning a court case against someone who copies it, spellings and all, for commercial gain. Call
your band The Associates, on the other hand, and your case
won't be as watertight.

THE MERCHANDISE

With record sales having slowed worldwide throughout the late
eighties and early nineties, bands which are able to keep on the
road have made up for lower record sales with the profits to be
had from merchandise. And it is often the cult acts which do
best where merchandising is concerned. In 1991 in the US, sales
of Morrisey t-shirts were greater than sales of U2 t-shirts; and
UK indie band Inspiral Carpets, which handles its own t-shirt
designs, has sold more t-shirts than records in its short history.
And when you consider that most t-shirts cost more than a CD,
yet most bands get a bigger cut from a t-shirt sale than they do
from a CD sale, you can see how important merchandising is
becoming in the nineties.

And of course a band can offer more than just t-shirts to adoring fans. Posters, photographs, dolls, badges, scarves and even underwear have all found favour with fans over the years.

THE MERCHANDISER AT WORK

There is no typical day, week or year for anyone in the music business, and the merchandiser is no exception. During a quiet period in which the merchandiser is pitching for new business a typical working week might involve the following tasks:

- Researching merchandising contracts being handled by rival companies, with a view to making an informed pitch to that rival's clients the next time around.

- Looking at new suppliers with a view to negotiating better deals on the manufacturing and delivery of merchandise with existing or new suppliers.

- Devising new merchandising ideas. The merchandising company with t-shirts and baseball caps is fine, but the band with the all-new merchandising gimmick is the band that will be remembered. It is of course impossible to apply a new idea to just any band or performer: all merchandising needs to be tailored to an act's image.

- Pitching to new clients. A merchandiser will always have an ear to the ground listening out for new tours in the offing. Contacts will need to be made and kept happy with the occasional lunch so that the merchandiser gets first word about a forthcoming tour. The merchandiser who gets in there first to pitch for a new job is going to stand the best chance, especially if he or she is armed with the right ideas for the act in question.

As work begins on a new contract, the merchandiser's tasks over a given period of time might include:

- meeting with artist and management to discuss merchandising design ideas;
- keeping in contact with the tour manager on the subject of venues – which venue, and when;
- liaising with venues on the subject of merchandising retail

positions;

- liaising with local police and councils to gain information on the piracy situation in the area;
- liaising with manufacturers on prices and delivery times.

THE JOBS

A big money business it may be, but merchandising employs few people. Although some bands have several t-shirt designs on the go at one time (UK indie darling Ned's Atomic Dustbin has over 30!), the work on offer to designers by merchandisers is limited.

And while in the past merchandisers would have needed teams of people to sell the gear at the gig, today, in the larger venues at least, that staff is provided.

So there are the designers and manufacturers (usually brought in for one-off jobs), the directors of the merchandising companies and the people who do the legwork – order the merchandise, control stock, deliver to venues, count the cash – and that's about it.

If merchandising appeals to you, your best bet is either to set up a small concern on your own and build on it or seek out the few large merchandising companies and drop them a line. Most in the business will advise, however, that self-starting is the best way in.

15

The fan club

Thinking of starting a fan club for you favourite band? Think again. We're not saying don't; just think again. Most fan clubs are started by fans and, believe it or not, however much a fan you are of anyone or anything at the moment, you may not be as passionate about the subject of your adoration in, say, 3 years' time.

There are exceptions to this general rule, of course. We've all seen the television documentaries and read the magazine articles about those who have remained devoted to the *King Of Rock And Roll* since they first heard him in the late fifties; how they've named their houses Gracelands, how their children are all called Elvis Aron, how they spend their annual holiday camped outside the real Gracelands and how every weekend is spent at a different Elvis convention. Such people make the job of running a fan club a truly pleasurable one. However, such people are also a rarity and even a dying breed.

Back to our warning: if you start a fan club in the heat of the moment, as a gesture of support for an act and its followers, the chances are that things will get out of hand, either because the act in question turns out to be a flash in the pan or because it turns out to be so huge that you suddenly find that you don't have the staff or the facilities to fulfil all the promises you made when you started the club in the first place.

So, think again, take a step backwards, and consider, firstly, what exactly a fan club is for.

WHAT ARE FAN CLUBS FOR?

A fan's yearning to live, eat and breathe the object of his or her desire is, for a short while, insatiable. Such fans want to know everything that is going on in at least the professional lives of their heroes, and they want to know it first. They also want to meet like-minded fans as, although their passion for the star might be extremely personal, most fans are extraordinarily generous to, and respectful of, those with whom they are forced to share their object of desire.

Fans meet up at concerts, often night after night, having come from all parts of the country, even the world, to see and hear their idols on stage. They cluster beforehand, comparing notes, discussing the last concert and anticipating the next. They swap photos, discuss rare recordings and, once the show starts, they delight in each other's pleasure. At their best, the subcultures which form around an artist or band are a joy to be a part of; there can be nothing more positive than a diverse group of people all brought together by a single love or passion.

Fan clubs usually come about to provide a focus for such a group of people. The motivation usually comes from the pleasure rather than the profit that's to be had from running such an organization – many who start fan clubs do so simply as a means by which to get as close as they possibly can to their idol. And if you can offer a service to all the above, artist or artists included, then you could find yourself having fun and being of use to people, all at the same time.

Once you've established your fan club's existence, however, those like-minded fans will want the earth from you. They will want constant updating on the whereabouts of their heroes; they'll want to know before anyone else when the next tour is and where it is going; and as fan club members they'll expect to be able to make priority bookings. Are you prepared for all this? Was this a spur of the moment idea which on reflection might be best left to those with more time, better financial security and at least some experience of running a business? Or are you still convinced that you are the best person to be running this fan club? If your answer to the last question is still yes, hold fire a little longer until we've looked in greater detail at what a fan club does.

STARTING A FAN CLUB

Many fan clubs are set up and run by those who are fans first and business people second, and as such many of these clubs survive for a comparatively short time. That so many such fan clubs enjoy a comparatively short life is not a surprising fact, however; nor is it necessarily a bad thing. After all, a person who has started a fan club out of sheer dedication to a particular act is as likely as any other person to lose some of that dedication as time passes, and then what will be the motivation to keep the fan club going? It's unlikely to be money as few fan clubs have ever made big profits; and to be fielding phone calls and answering letters from the desperate fans of an act for whom your passion is wilting might prove too much to handle. This is the time either to close down the fan club or hand over the running of the club to somebody else. But before you do that, we'll take a look at what the running of this club entails.

Before you start

Wherever your support and backing comes from, you are advised to consider exactly what sort of service you hope your fan club will be able to offer *before* you consider asking for members to commit a membership fee. At this stage you should ask yourself the following questions:

- Is this just an information service, or will I be offering other services and products such as an information line, a discount and/or priority ticket service, t-shirts, photographs on request, a magazine, conventions or other similar events?

- Am I doing this alone? Do I want to be paid for my services? If I get help can I afford to pay for it?

- If I'm receiving subscriptions, do I need a bank account? If so, is it too risky to use my own? Should I set up a separate bank account? Do I need to be able to accept credit cards and, if so, how is this arranged? If I'm working with a management or record company, could I use its bank account, and if I were to do this could I be ripped off? Would the management or record company expect a cut? Do I need to register for VAT? Should I get an accountant?

- At what price should I set the subscription? Under what conditions should it be refundable? Should I collect it yearly, half-yearly, quarterly or monthly?

- How many letters am I likely to receive on a daily or weekly basis once the fan club has been established? Should I answer unsolicited letters? When and how often would I do this? Who would pay for the postage?

- Will I get the artist's support and cooperation? How do I set about this?

- Do I still want to do it?

Publicity

Once the decision has been made to set up a fan club, it then has to be publicized. If the act in question has a strong live following or is particularly popular at this time then the most effective method of publicizing the enterprise, through the distribution of leaflets, or *leafleting*, will be comparatively simple. Leafleting can be done at gigs, inside record sleeves and t-shirts (if the record company/management/merchandising company/production department approve and cooperate) or through direct mail. Your mailing list could be acquired from the record and/or management company if either or both have been wise enough to log the names and addresses that appear on fan mail. Otherwise, every cheap form of advertising you know of will have to be employed.

Here you have your first major expense. If you are setting up the club in association with a record or management company and with the approval and support of the act in question, the people working in these organizations may help you finance the printing of the leaflets, in full or in part, and will certainly have printers and designers on hand who will be able to produce them quickly and cheaply. The act's management will also be able to see to it that leaflets are distributed at live concerts.

If the record company and/or management are really keen to get involved they might even suggest placing an advertisement in a magazine or music paper that is read by fans of the band in question. This would certainly give your fan club credibility and could well find you more subscribers than you are prepared to handle.

If you are setting up the club independently, on the other hand, you will have to find the publicity money yourself, and neither the printing of leaflets nor the placing of press advertisements comes cheap. If you are working on a shoestring and without the support of an organization linked to the band in question, you are advised to keep costs low from the outset, perhaps relying at the beginning on word of mouth for publicity, through the existing network of fans (with which you will of course have contact, being a fan yourself). Also, as long as you have record company and management approval, the fans will always eventually find you. There is, after all, no more resourceful person than a desperate fan. One look at the inner sleeve of an album or CD will give fans the name of both the management and the record company, and one call to directory enquiries will give them the phone numbers of both. And you can be guaranteed that both management and record company will be more than happy to refer these calling fans on to you.

Making promises

What will the leaflets be telling the fans? It's important here that you don't promise what you can't deliver. A quarterly magazine? A telephone information service? Exclusive tour information? And all for, say, a £15 annual subscription?

Note this true-life cautionary tale. This UK band was one of the biggest of the eighties. It had a massive following of mainly, but not exclusively, young girls – and its members had a very sympathetic attitude to their fans. The band encouraged the setting up of a fan club, at its management offices, and even contributed to the start-up costs. Needless to say, the subscription cheques came pouring in, and as would happen with any sensible business these cheques were banked immediately. The problem was that none of the management staff had anticipated the size of the response, and it soon proved impossible to deal with all the subscriptions and run the management company at the same time. Fans waited by the letter box for weeks hoping to receive their membership numbers, letters of introduction and all the other membership privileges offered in return for subscriptions, but few received anything.

Soon the parents of the disappointed fans began to get

involved and the band suddenly faced a potential scandal. As no fraud was intended and the fan club had been started with the best of intentions, it was decided by both band and management that the fan club would have to be closed down. Those fans which had not received anything for their money had it refunded, and many of these refunds were paid for from band members' own pockets. A sad tale with a reasonably happy ending in the sense that at least nobody ended up in court and no innocent fan was left out of pocket. Not all such situations can be resolved in this way, however.

THE FANZINE

The most useful and the most lucrative service you can offer fellow fans is a *fanzine*. Fanzine readers are generally more than happy to put up with fairly basic presentation, with many very successful fanzines offering little more than a series of typed and photocopied A4 pages stapled together.

It's the information that counts – that, plus the words of other like-minded fans which often make up the pages of a fanzine. Fanzine editors who are regularly in touch with the act concerned are often able to offer tour news and other facts and figures long before they reach the national and international music press. Fanzines can also serve fans of bands who don't make the music press either because they are out of fashion or because they are of such a minority interest that the mainstream music press simply won't touch them.

Endorsement by the subject of the fanzine isn't necessary for a publication to be successful, but such an endorsement might lend it extra credibility among potential readers. Artist approval is likely also to mean artist cooperation; offers of signed photos and even CDs as competition prizes can help to boost circulation, as can exclusive interviews and backstage photographs.

Publishing a fanzine

Most fans will pay £1+ for a decent fanzine of eight pages or more. Presuming you're writing it all yourself and/or using unpaid fans as contributors (we wouldn't recommend a slave labour policy, but it happens) your fanzine could soon be in small profit. This would leave funds for improvement, better quality design or even a circulation drive! There are existing fanzines, in the US in particular, which have done so well that they are now properly printed and bound with photographs inside and even a cover in colour! Such a presentation will of course encourage advertising, and before you know it, you're a publisher!

To get an idea of how a fanzine is put together, it's worth studying as many examples as you can get your hands on. No wonderful desktop publishing system is required for the beginner; a typewriter and a creative mind will do to start with. Some fanzines are handwritten. This is a cheap but time-consuming way of putting a publication together, although in some cases the handwritten look can actually give added appeal.

You would advertise your fanzine in the same way as you would a complete fan club service (see above); leafleting and distribution could happen at gigs, and again if your fanzine is endorsed by the artist and record company word of mouth will soon ensure that die-hard fans hear about it.

Again, avoid the dangers of taking and banking money for subscriptions you can't honour.

THE CONVENTION

An established fan club with a following, reasonable financial backing and a good mailing list is in a good position to establish a regular convention in honour of the subjects of their adoration. Beach Boys and Beatles conventions are still well attended the world over even today, and other smaller events celebrating lesser known acts happen all the time, often remaining a well kept secret to all but die-hard fans.

People will pay reasonable sized entrance fees if a convention promises a reasonable calibre of guest (surprise appearances by the artists themselves, if they're still alive, will always help the attendance figures for your next convention!). Other tried-and-tested convention attractions include good merchandising and record stalls (Chapter 14), live performances (by soundalikes or spin-off acts), guest speakers with links to the artist in question and a good DJ.

A strong convention attendance could well put you in profit, although the obvious pitfalls, such as hiring too expensive a venue and paying too high fees for appearances, should be anticipated and avoided.

It is important to remember in the case of all such enterprises that normal rules apply: if your fanzine, your convention or your fan club activities put you in profit, you will have to pay tax on those profits; if you hire a hall you will need insurance, and so on. Fan clubs, fanzines and conventions are all businesses and the rules governing business are tight. So read up on those rules and ask advice every step of the way if you're going to avoid all the pitfalls which so many small businesses suffer.

SETTING UP ON YOUR OWN

As has just been stated, understanding tax, insurance, bookkeeping and all the other basics of business is crucial if you're planning to set up a small fan club enterprise on your own. As soon as you start taking money from people in return for a promised service or product, you are entering into a contract, and there are strict laws governing all types of contract.

Legal and financial advice will be invaluable if you are planing to go ahead with such an enterprise; such advice may slow you down and cost you money at the start, but it will almost definitely stand you in good stead when things get off the ground and the money starts flowing, because it is then when, if you're not careful, you can suddenly find yourself in trouble.

TAKING THE SAFE ROUTE

With merchandising now a significant earner in the music business, many merchandising companies are finding that to run a fan club or information service (which also happens to make merchandise available, by mail order for example) can provide them with another outlet for their merchandise.

There are therefore now a number of merchandising companies which also offer skeleton fan services. These services are rarely of the personal kind which fan-run organizations often offer and may simply be little more than glorified mail order businesses.

Such organizations may be in a position to offer employment, but will rarely be offering large salaries. They can be traced via any merchandise you might purchase at record shops or concerts.

Otherwise, few fan clubs or fanzines employ anyone full time, and so the job prospects in this area of the music business are slim. Running your own fan club or fanzine successfully, however, could well stand you in good stead for a job in a music management or record company, or perhaps a job with a music paper, particularly if your fanzine gathers respect for its coverage and editorial style.

16

The artist

The would-be artists are the only people referred to in this book who will be affected by the actions of everyone else mentioned for the duration of their careers.

If the manager's no good, the artist suffers. If the concert promoter's no good, the artist suffers. If the record company's no good, the artist suffers. If the tour manager, the plugger or publisher are no good, the artist suffers. If the A&R person's no good, the artist suffers; in fact if the A&R person's no good the artist might never have been discovered in the first place. And so on, and so on.

It works the other way around too, of course: if the artists are no good, then all the above are likely to go down with them. The artists and the material they write and perform are at the hub of the music business.

But before we burden all aspiring artists with such a responsibility, it is important to remember that most musicians, singers and bands never reach the dizzy heights of international stardom; many don't want this, few are ever able to attain it anyway and most are happy making a reasonable living doing what they love: playing their instruments, singing their songs and getting applause and hopefully money at the end of it all.

In fact, many of the best-paid artists and performers in the music business are those you have never heard of: the session musicians, the behind-the-scenes writers, the cabaret stars who make fortunes around the world but whose chart careers were either very brief or never existed. The music business has much to offer the artist in terms of both money and job satisfaction. It is important from the outset, however, for artists to decide what their goals are and try as best they can to keep their aims straight.

HOW HIGH ARE YOU AIMING?

Many people when they start out are aiming for the top. This is natural, because most of the people who have been their inspiration will be those they have heard on record or seen on the television or live on stage. There is very often one single experience which turns a person into an aspiring rock star: many of today's established rock stars talk of the first time they ever heard a particular band or singer. If an artist is inspired by a huge star, it's difficult for that artist not to set his or her sights as high.

For people who are aiming high, however, there is no question about the dedication that will be required; they will have to live, breathe, eat, sleep and drink their art. They will have to work harder than anyone else at it; if you want to be the world's most successful guitarist, you will have to be the world's most hard-working guitarist. And so on. Rather than stressing in this book the level of dedication required, we suggest that all aspiring superstars get hold of three or four biographies of superstars, just to get an idea of exactly how hard those people had to work to get there and what they lost of their normal lives along the way.

STARTING OUT

If you want to be in a band, then you need two things: a band and something to contribute to that band. Traditionally, embryonic rock and pop bands have most difficulty finding drummers and lead singers. So, if you are one such person, you're likely to find it's a seller's market out there. If you are a lone musician or singer, or even songwriter, looking for a band to play with, you'll find ads in the classified sections of most music papers and other specialist magazines aimed at musicians or those working in showbusiness generally. Joining a band as a stranger answering an advertisement can be an intimidating experience. The chances are that the other band members have been together for a while, will have their own idiosyncratic ways of playing, their own private jokes and maybe a slight if unintentional hostility towards the new unknown. Fear not in this situation, however. There's nothing like playing in a band for binding people together. If you gel as musicians, things will work out even if your social lives continue to take different paths.

If you are simply part of a band which has come together organically – no recruitment needed, you were all together anyway – you could well have the perfect basis on which to commit 100% to the cause of making it big. You're all friends, so no one's missing out socially even were you to work through the night to get a particular song or lyric right. But beware. You may have all been together as kids, but you will all grow up, and growing up can mean growing apart. Few bands stay together for 30 years: The Rolling Stones are an exception. Read one or two of the biographies of that band that are around and you'll understand why.

And what of the lone singer? Can you name any of today's current successes who were always alone? Take a random selection – from Bjork to Annie Lennox, from Elton John to Bobby Brown, from Sting to Michael Jackson, from Madonna to Kate Bush. They all started out in bands, except for Kate Bush. She was the exception whose journey to stardom was one of which dreams are made. She was discovered while still at school by Pink Floyd guitar supremo and producer Dave Gilmour who paid for her to make some demos which in turn won her a contract with EMI. How many others can tell such a story?

No, we're back to the hard slog. Even a solo artist who has total confidence in his or her talents would be well advised to join a band and tread the boards for a few years. Get some experience of working with musicians and shining above them, for that's what makes a solo star, and of facing and working an audience. Then break away. But time your breakaway carefully; it doesn't always work.

GETTING NOTICED

There are three main stages to the careers ahead of most aspiring bands, singers and musicians – making it on the live circuit, making it on record and making it internationally – and it usually happens in that order. Many won't be aiming much past stage 1, and will be happy as a session player (Chapter 18) on some sort of cabaret circuit at a professional or semiprofessional level, playing and or singing with one or more acts and maybe occasionally contributing to a recording.

To achieve regular work on the live circuit you will need to watch out for ads in the music press for vacancies within bands, and if you already have a band, or a self-sufficient solo act, you will need to start contacting booking agents. This can be done in a number of ways, and one way would be to make a list of the sorts of venue you would like to play, maybe within a 15- or 20-mile radius of your base to begin with, and find out where those venues obtain their acts. These venues may well seek out their acts themselves, but others will use booking agents, who will charge you the performer, not the venue, for having got you the gig.

The booking agent

There are things to watch out for in an agent. Does the agent really understand what type of act you are? Will he or she find you the right gigs? Are you a *priority* act for the agent or do you exist on the agent's books simply as a filler should your type of band be needed to satisfy a particular customer? Are you working for the agent or is the agent working for you? The agent should be working for you, because it's you who pays the agent, usually 15% of your night's earnings. At the early stages of your career, when you may be getting £25 a night or even less for a whole band an agent may not be interested. After all, 15% of £25 is £3.75! In such a situation you will most likely be touting around for gigs yourselves; get to know the clubs and pubs which take on bands like yours and ask for an audition (some places run these regularly, often in front of an audience!) or play them a demo tape.

Later, when you are in a position to use an agent, ensure that the agent sticks to the two most important rules in the book as far as artists are concerned: that the fee is not more than 15% and that you are paid your share on the night immediately after the gig, or as soon after that time as possible. Such is the insistence of the two key agents' organizations in the UK – The Agents' Association of Great Britain and the National

Entertainment Agents Council. These would be worth contacting if you're looking for an agent or, indeed, should you wish to become an agent yourself.

The manager

The manager's job is discussed at some length in Chapter 4. From the artist's point of view, however, finding, or being found by, the right manager can straighten the path to success, but it can also do the opposite. As we have warned would-be managers to think twice when asked to take on the role by a young act, similarly we would warn aspiring artists to avoid being flattered by the first whizz-kid who comes along offering to be their guide and mentor. A good manager can certainly get the best out of a bad act, but a bad manager can ruin the chances forever of an act which might otherwise have had potential. Think carefully about what a manager should be doing for you and whether, in the early stages of your career, you actually need one. And beware signing anything in a rush, too. A mere 15% of our aforementioned £25 gig fee may seem like peanuts to be paying a manager for getting you the gig (often the manager will do this instead of the agent), but when that 15% becomes 15% of everything you earn, whether the manager was involved or not, that's when the court cases start, careers are put on hold and you lose it.

On the other hand, it could be down to the manager's skill that you win the coveted record deal which gives you a better percentage (see below) than you ever expected. In which case does that manager not deserve a good cut for ever more? These are the sorts of question the aspiring artist should be considering at the outset in order to ensure that things don't get nasty later on.

A&R

So you've been playing a few gigs and by now you might even have a manager or management company (Chapter 4) working for you. As a solo performer or band you should now know which way you're headed. If you intend to remain on the live circuit as a show act, you will be wanting to polish up your act and your appearance and move into higher calibre venues that pay high calibre fees. The right manager, convinced of your talent, will work with you towards this goal.

If, on the other hand, your next goal is a recording contract, you and your manager should now be looking towards the A&R departments (Chapter 7) of the record companies (Chapter 3).

At this stage of your career, a good manager will be channelling most effort into sounding out the A&R people. A management company with good A&R contacts will be better at this than a first-time manager whose skills are growing with you. However, it will be aggression and determination that will win through here, whatever experience in the business you and your manager have had up until now. After all, finding out the names of the key A&R people at the record companies you are targeting is not a difficult job, and no A&R person worth his or her salt will ignore any call. Approaches by managers might be prioritized and yours may be bottom of the list for a long time, but it would be stupid to ignore your manager altogether.

You may or may not have a demo tape. This will be down to money, but it is an essential tool in the chasing of A&R people. As we have explained in Chapter 7, the A&R person might listen to a few seconds and then place it straight into your s.a.e. (after rewinding it, of course); to avoid this happening it might be wiser to get the A&R person down to the gig. This is never easy, and you and your management might want to consider all sorts of gimmicks to attract attention. Getting a support gig with an upcoming act is not a bad idea; sending elaborate invitations of the kind an A&R person could not forget; busking outside the record companies' offices (Elvis Costello tried that one and look where he is now) – all these things are worth a try. However, making a name for yourselves on the live circuit through word of mouth is the sure way of getting the A&R people to fight over you. An act that can fill venues wherever it goes, particularly if it is playing its own material, is an A&R person's dream come true. Why? Because it proves the material exists and is listenable; it proves the act can cut it on stage; and it proves that it must have some kind of workable image. Otherwise people wouldn't be going back to see this act over and over again, and paying for the privilege.

Once an A&R person has shown an interest, now is the time to be on your guard. You'd be wise to try and play one off against the other because there are tricks the A&R people play which can land you in trouble. For example, it can be very flattering to be invited into the studio by an A&R person to make a demo, all expenses paid by the record company, of course. They must be interested, you think to yourselves. Why else would they be spending all this money on us? The answer to this question is that they might be spending all this money on you to keep you temporarily off the market. If there are other A&R people after you at the time, this could allow them to lose interest in you (they think you're going for another deal), thus lowering your market price. Keeping you in a demo studio might also give the record company just enough time to research the market properly and decide at the end that you're not right for them. This could have a devastating effect on your recording career. So beware.

Not all A&R people operate in this devious way, and we have to presume that the A&R people who have shown an interest in you are now about to sign you up.

HOW GOOD ARE YOU?

Who can ever say but an audience? Playing live will always serve as the best way of gauging how good you are as a performer or group of performers. Audiences go back time and time again to see a good act, however well known or otherwise it may be. If you ever get to the point where every house you play is full, you can rest assured that you're doing something right. Talent scouts from all areas of the music business, too, will always show enthusiasm for an act that goes down well live in front of an audience.

Otherwise, how do you know how good you are? Once you've signed a deal, be it a management, publishing or recording deal, or all three, there will be people with a vested interest in how you look and sound, and they will be on hand to tell you where you're going wrong and, more importantly, where you're going right. Before that, though, it is up to yourself as an artist or part of a group of artists to be as self-critical (not self-destructive) as you feel is necessary in order to get your act as good as it can be. But what is good and what is otherwise is always a subjective judgement, particularly in popular music. All musicians and singers know how technically good they are, but in pop, technical proficiency is only the half of it. Less than half, in many cases. How you judge the other fifty or so per cent is really one of the great mysteries of rock and roll. Nobody can teach you that, and that's why those who do find it often reap great rewards.

THE PUBLISHER

Before we move on to the deal, a word about the publisher (Chapter 5). If as a solo act or as a band you have proved you can write songs you might be ripe for a deal with a publisher even before anyone shows an interest in you as a recording act. In this case the publisher could well be the person to get you your deal as he or she will have record company contacts and might even be prepared to invest money in you by paying for a decent demo. Let us presume that either through manager and A&R or publisher and A&R, or through some other miraculous method (making your own dance records for example and getting them played by a top club DJ or two), you manage to find a record company willing to sign you up. What happens next?

THE DEAL

Many acts will live or die by this deal, so here is the moment at which you put aside all the euphoria, the hopes, the dreams, the rock and roll attitude and you sit down with manager, lawyer (Chapter 6), A&R people and record company legal department and thrash it out.

Artist's royalties in the UK vary from 10% to 15% of the record's retail price (excluding VAT). They are paid on each record sold, and it is these which are negotiable at the time of signing the contract. Negotiations will include how the royalties are split between the rest of the band. Writers will also receive *mechanicals* and *performing rights* payments (Chapter 17); these are fixed and only vary according to the deal with your publisher.

The advance

The deal you sign with the record company will determine not only your royalty rate but also your initial advance. The advance is a lump sum usually administered by your manager to pay for equipment, recording fees, wages and tax, if you're sensible. All advances will be recouped against royalties, in other words an advance is a loan repayable by your earnings from record sales, so a big advance doesn't necessarily mean you're rich! Many a band's contract has expired with its members owing the record company money, and record companies will want this money back somehow, so beware the lure of the big advance.

WHERE TO NEXT?

A leader (or occasionally a couple of leaders) usually emerge early on in a band's life, and these roles will often become crystallized in the studio. The studio will offer an environment and a way of working for which few will be prepared. Engineers and producers will warm to the communicative ones in the band, and the others (often the *back line*) could become isolated if all concerned fail to apply some diplomacy and democracy. There will always be band members who prefer to lead and band members who prefer to be led; this balance can provide the perfect working environment as long as all are agreed on their roles.

Recording an album can be a joyful experience, and usually will be first time around, especially if you have the right producer, the A&R people are happy with the material and the signs are that the record company is going to put its weight behind the finished product.

Then will come the real work: the promoting, the touring, the build-up to the second album, the holding of the whole thing together after having already achieved so much of what you originally set out to do. If your vision was narrow and you were only ever looking a year or two ahead – to the first big gig or the first album – the next few years' work will be tough for you. If this was a life plan, on the other hand, you're now in the perfect position to reach for the stars.

17

The songwriter

Few generalizations can be made about the job of the song-writer. No two songwriters write in the same way; no two song-writers earn the same amount of money for their work; and songwriters cannot predict how much they might earn this year or the next, or can ever guarantee that, as from tomorrow, they will ever earn a single penny from their craft again. As a song-writer you can earn vast sums of money, but you can also hit the lowest lows the music business has to offer.

Songwriting is pretty well the only job in the business in which you have to start from scratch with every project. A gui-tarist can buy a better guitar, take tips from fellow guitarists, develop an on-stage style and, with practice, will almost always improve from one day to the next. A manager can mould and develop an act and learn and develop management skills as the act grows in stature and in confidence. Publishers and A&R people will learn from experience how to find, how to nurture and how to sell their acts and their properties, and producers are learning new tricks of the trade all the time – often aided by new technology which is racing ahead of every other trend in the business.

Meanwhile, having finished one song, the songwriter moves to the next one facing the same blank sheet of paper, facing the same fears over whether or not the publisher, the manager and the band will like or even understand this next piece of work, and facing the frustrating fact that no one, least of all the song-writer, knows how or when the next song will be complete and, when it is complete, whether it will be usable. A songwriter is only as good as his or her last song. That's the sad fact of the songwriter's lot.

It's not all bad, however, and there are some lessons that can be learned by songwriters; there are some tools at the songwriter's disposal too. So to begin with, we'll consider the songwriter's craft. Is it one which can be learned?

STARTING OUT

There are certain rules that the songwriter can follow, particularly if the goal is a hit pop song. The perfect hit pop song, for example, has a very definite structure to it. It will always have a verse, a catchy chorus, a *middle-eight* or a *bridge* to break up the song and possibly build to a key change, and a climactic ending or a fade. It will usually last around 3 minutes and will be fairly up-beat, or at least will have a regular rhythm.

However, simply to follow this structure is usually not enough. Many have stuck rigidly to the pop formula but failed consistently to come up with a memorable or a saleable song. Moreover, many of the truly memorable and high-earning pop songs of the last 30 or so years have been those which have broken all these rules and more. Take The Beatles' Eleanor Rigby for example, or Queen's Bohemian Rhapsody. The former dispensed with regulation guitar, bass and drums line-up and opted instead for a string quartet; the latter lasted closer to 9 minutes, its tempo wandered all over the place and much of it was closer to opera than pop. Yet both are today regarded as popular music classics. With rules as bendable as this, it can be hard for the aspiring writer to know where to start. On the other hand, if all the rules are breakable, or at least bendable, surely this means that pop songwriters can go wherever their minds take them?

The truth of the matter is that there never were any rules. There was a time, before the sixties singer–songwriter/pop group boom, during which songwriters were employed to churn out songs almost on demand by publishers and record companies, and in this way certain formulas did develop. But after The Beatles in the UK and Bob Dylan in the US, any writer's rule books that might have existed went out of the window.

Today, particularly in the UK, writers in the pop genre tend to develop within groups. They may write alone but they usually know who they're writing for in terms of both their audience and the people who will be singing and playing the songs. Take pretty well any big band of the nineties – from REM to Guns'n'Roses, from The Pet Shop Boys to U2 – and you'll find that the people who write their songs are also prominent band members. Many of the world's top solo stars in the pop field are also the writers of their own material – from Elton John to Sting, from Madonna to Michael Jackson and from Van Morrison to Bruce Springsteen.

So here emerges perhaps one of the most important questions that today's aspiring songwriters should be asking themselves: who is going to be performing my work?

PERFORMERS OR SONGS?

Which comes first, the chicken or the egg, the performers or the songs? In the case of many established bands, the songwriting came later. Such was the case with The Beatles (even though Paul McCartney was writing songs from the age of 13) and more particularly with The Rolling Stones. As pioneer singer–songwriters, these two bands got together at the outset because of a shared love of a type of music; with The Beatles it was rock and roll and with The Stones it was the blues. Both bands started out by playing the music of their idols and only after some success did they begin seriously to start working on their own compositions. So this is an important consideration to make when starting out as a writer; do you first establish a group of musicians within which you can develop your song-writing skills or do you develop them alone and hope to find later those people who will play them? Or, indeed, should you simply perform them yourself as a solo artist?

THE NON-POP SONG

You may, of course, not wish to follow the pop path. Perhaps you're more interested in classical music, film music, music for television, radio jingles, folk songs or club-oriented dance music. In all of these cases you stand more of a chance of making a name for yourself (though not necessarily much money) simply because each represents a specialist area and therefore there is less competition and a tighter and more manageable network of people to get to know.

Folk, jazz, country & western

If you write in either of these genres you would clearly want to work to get on the right club circuit. Your local what's on guide would tell you where and when your local folk, jazz and country & western (C&W) clubs are, and if you're any good (as a performer) getting to know local club managers will eventually get you a gig. If you're a writer but not a performer you would need to befriend the musicians themselves; by the very nature of these musical styles the musicians are approachable and not all write their own songs, so the chances of getting one of yours tried out are good. From here on it's up to you. There are specialist labels and publishers serving these musical styles, and most of them are comparatively accessible in the same way as the artists are. The growing network you are establishing via the clubs you visit will eventually lead you to the right people. Then your songs will do the work for you.

Jingles

If writing jingles or music for commercials is your passion, then getting to know commercials production houses through advertising agencies is your way forward. The agencies will give you names and addresses of these houses – where the actual commercials are made – and then it is up to you to make them aware of your talents. The agencies might take a shine to your work (you should have a demo tape to play to people) and might recommend you to a particular production house they use themselves. Such a recommendation will always be taken seriously.

As an aspiring jingle writer you should be attempting to record as many examples of your work as possible; here, essential tools of the trade will include recording equipment (possibly even a portable studio) and a synthesizer, which together would allow you (and an accomplice perhaps?) to overlay a number of different instrumental parts in order to develop and demonstrate your ideas. These tapes should be taken around to ad agencies, production houses, independent television production companies, television continuity departments and radio stations, day-in, day-out.

It should be noted that the jingles business is very tough to break into. Another way in would be through companies who specialize in *library* music, which can be used by people working in all audiovisual media, from slide-tape training presentations to network radio and television.

Make a nuisance of yourself until someone says 'yes' just to shut you up. It does work that way sometimes! Jingles are an integral part of today's mass media, and the more you know and understand the workings of those media, the better a position you will be in to exploit your talents.

Film

If your ambition is to write film music then it's likely you will have studied composition at college, as to construct perhaps an hour's worth or more of themed incidental music requires considerably more technical know-how than is needed for the jingle or the 3-minute pop song. You will want to meet people who write and produce film music; you would benefit greatly from working in studios where film music is performed, often live, in front of a projected silent cut of the final film; you will want to meet film producers, directors and sound engineers; you might want to catch them early and get to know them while they're still at film school. A spell at film school yourself could be beneficial, too; specialize in music while you're there and the people who graduate with you as producers or directors might well stick with you later in life.

Formal musical training along with the opportunity to live and breathe the film industry for a while – an opportunity you're going to have to make for yourself – would provide a sound background for an aspiring film music writer.

Work in television could lead you on to film; the two industries are increasingly interlinked, so contact with a number of the many independent television production companies could serve to point you in the right direction. As with the film companies it is the producers and the executive producers you will need to win to get your music considered. Working your way in via the studios which record film music could serve as a route to the right people, too. Engineering or production skills would serve you well here (Chapter 8).

Dance

The dance music explosion of the late eighties, which has shown no signs of dying off in the nineties, has provided work and exposure for a whole range of people who might never have enjoyed such hands-on experience in the close-knit, elitist pop music business of the sixties, seventies and early eighties.

There are still those who hail punk as the genre that opened up the music business to the ordinary man and woman in the street, killed off the rock dinosaurs of the early seventies and offered popular music a new foundation on which to build a leaner, more credible industry.

Others would argue that punk merely got the industry's businessmen and women wise to some of the silly record deals that artists were being offered then and that it is the technology-aided dance boom that has really allowed the young person in his or her bedroom to make it on to vinyl when, just a few year's back, to do so would have been an unattainable dream.

Computer-aided writing and recording has allowed people to create (that can mean write and record, almost simultaneously) their own dance tracks and get them pressed up as vinyl 12" discs and into the hands of the club DJs in a very short time – and at comparatively little cost. These records might not sell in vast numbers, but then again they might. They certainly stand a strong chance of getting played in a club somewhere, particularly if you spend the rest of your time *networking* with the DJs who matter in your area. And to see a crowd respond to one or your own creations provides the best incentive anyone could need to go back and do more.

Classical

While success in the above fields can be won by a combination of networking, pushiness, luck, being in the right place at the right time and the two elements common to all, absolute determination and hard work, success in the classical field will depend much more on the last two elements than on any of the others.

The reasons for this are many, and one of the most important is the fact that classical music is not tied up with prevailing fashions (that's not to say that classical music doesn't have its trends, of course). The 3-minute pop song or the advertising jingle can be polished off fast and targeted quickly through existing, highly efficient infrastructures which respond to rapidly changing social and economic trends. If properly packaged and targeted in response to a particular trend, a pop single and its follow-up album can sell hundreds of thousands and even millions of units in a very short period of time. Classical music, and particularly new classical music, rarely does this.

Needless to say, as the music business becomes increasingly sophisticated, so tried-and-tested classics are increasingly being repackaged and marketed along popular music lines, but this doesn't help the aspiring classical composer. The aspiring classical composer will be influenced and affected, and possibly will have his or her career largely carved out by, the classical music establishment of the time. Promising writers and performers in the classical field are usually *discovered* while they are studying their craft, by teachers and others who have connections with a particular music college. Concerts will be staged, in which student composers' pieces will be played by student performers, and the right people will be invited. Those people might be record company bosses, radio producers, orchestra directors or organizers of classical music competitions. It is through these competitions incidentally (there are many which carry considerable prestige) that many aspiring performers and composers come to national and international attention. Before you get into any of this, however, there's one crucial skill to be learned, that of being able to score a piece of music.

So with the classics, the message is *listen to your teachers.*

EARNING FROM WRITING

Songwriting has made millionaires of many. It has also been the ruin of many. Such is the nature of songwriting that it has its ups and downs whether you're a success or otherwise. The greatest songwriters in the world – from Bacharach to Bono – have had their fair share of failures, and when one comes along it can immediately cause them to question their abilities. So be heartened; all the greats, all your heroes, have been through that agonizing period of self-doubt, often many times over. The fact that they have made millions from work they've done in the past is of course some comfort, and is a comfort which most aspiring songwriters will never have. Nonetheless, you *can* earn from your craft, and here are some of the ways this can be done.

COPYRIGHT

As a composer in the UK, your music is protected under the Copyright Designs and Patents Act of 1988. This act basically says that as soon as you have recorded your work, either on tape, on computer disk or on paper, it is then under copyright. To protect this copyright and/or to prove your copyright, you should then post a copy of your tape, disk or manuscript to yourself by registered mail, writing the name of the works on the outside of the envelope. This should then remain in a safe place, ideally with your solicitor's signature written over the seal of the envelope. This does not create a copyright, but simply gives evidence as to when the copyright work was created, which can be helpful if there is ever a dispute over breach of copyright in later years.

If you write songs in partnership, with one other person or with a band, it is as well to state the proportion of ownership of copyright at this stage, with all parties signing in agreement.

The more songs you copyright in this way, the more likely it is that you'll benefit from an *assignment of rights* with a publisher (Chapter 5). Don't just hand over your copyright to the first publisher who promises the earth; take advice from other songwriters, publishers, the Mechanical Copyright Protection Society (MCPS), the Performing Rights Society, the British Academy of Songwriters, Composers and Authors (BASCA; see below) and a solicitor before going ahead.

Royalties

As already discussed in Chapter 5, the MCPS in the UK (like Broadcast Music Inc. in the US) licenses companies and individuals who record its members' copyright musical works and collects and distributes to those owners the royalties payable under those licences. If as a writer you have a publisher, then it is your publisher who should be a member of the MCPS, and the publisher will in turn pass on these royalties to you after first taking a cut. Alternatively, you can join yourself as a composer–member. It will cost you nothing, but there will be a commission of between 5% and 15% taken on your royalties.

As also discussed in Chapter 5, royalties are also payable to the copyright owner every time his or her song is performed or broadcast in public. These royalties are collected in the form of licence fees by the Performing Rights Society (PRS) in the UK and the American Society of Composers, Authors and Publishers (ASCAP) in the US. The PRS grants licences to a variety of venues, including clubs, pubs and supermarkets, and radio and television companies, and distributes the fees collected from these venues to its members. As a composer you can apply for membership (at a cost of £50) if you have had three works which have been

- commercially recorded;

- broadcast in the past 2 years;

- performed in public on at least 12 occasions in the past 2 years and commercially published.

If you don't or can't join the PRS but have a publishing deal, you will benefit from your publisher's PRS membership, once PRS has taken its 18% and your publisher his or her 10–20%.

BASCA

Formerly known as The Songwriters' Guild, The British Academy of Songwriters, Composers and Authors (BASCA) is an organization which all aspiring writers are advised to contact as it exists to give advice and information to songwriters on all aspects of the music business. BASCA campaigns for the use of British songs and music in all of the media and organizes the prestigious songwriting awards events the Gold Badge Awards and the Ivor Novello Awards.

BASCA holds regular surgeries and seminars at which aspiring songwriters can learn from those who have succeeded in the business. All would-be songwriters are eligible for membership.

18

The session player

Next time you watch a television performance by an internationally successful solo artist, take your eyes off the star for a moment and check out the people in the band. A few top-name solo acts will have a permanent band, but most backing bands will be staffed by session musicians.

As you watch them play you'll notice several differences between these players and those who play regularly with the same band. The session players will often look neater, tidier, fitter and certainly more relaxed than the average band member, and the reasons for this are many. The main reason though is that unlike the regular members of an established band, who have been together since school and who have seen the hardship of the road, who have fallen in and out of love with each other and whose individual careers might not stand any great chance were the band to split, the session musicians have a life outside any given band they might find themselves with.

Successful session musicians (and in the term session musician we include session singers) go to sleep at night having done a job of work they know they'll be paid for. They get up in the morning in their own homes and set off for work (wherever that might be that day) just like anyone else. And they go to work because they've been asked for – sometimes by a band or singer, a *fixer* (see below) or a producer. They play because they love playing; they get the chance to play with a wide range of different people and, if they don't like a particular producer, band or singer, they can say 'no'. They also don't suffer the stresses and strains of stardom.

The picture painted here is of course somewhat idyllic and not necessarily a description of a typical session player. However, a session musician who is successful and in demand can enjoy much of the best that the music business has to offer a musician, can choose when and with whom to play and is not reliant on the sustained popularity of a particular band or type of music.

The session player does of course have to have something to offer in return for this appealing way of life, and that usually comes in the form of technical excellence combined with an efficient approach to work or a unique, distinctive style which will give a special gloss to the finished product. The two combined would make for a most highly prized session player. However, the latter quality tends to be found in *star name players*: the value a Stevie Wonder harmonica solo or a Mark Knopfler guitar break can add to a recording is immeasurable. These two and other such virtuosos will usually only play sessions for their friends (and this is often done for nothing!) or their heroes. Even a fixer with an open-ended budget wouldn't be able to persuade such talent into a session unless there was something other than money to be gained by that player making an appearance.

Session people must have more to offer, in terms of musical know-how and professionalism, than the regular band member. For example, everyone acknowledges the unique talent of Rolling Stone guitarist Keith Richards. How many are aware, however, that many of those memorable guitar licks took hours and sometimes even days to perfect? While a permanent line-up can spend open-ended amounts of time together rehearsing and developing styles and techniques, a paid-for session player will always be expected to deliver pretty well straight away. That's what the successful session player will always be able to offer, and will be paid well for it.

TRAINING REQUIRED

Most working session players will have had some form of musical training, and will have taken that training on into some sort of further education – at music college, academy or university. Such a background will not only guarantee the ability to play at least one instrument to professional standards but will also mean that the musician concerned will be able to read music or *sight read*. Many fixers and producers insist on this, although not all do. There are those players whose name or style would so enhance a piece of music that they are allowed to bring their own methods into the recording studio, however unorthodox they might be.

Having been through a formal musical training and presumably having acquired some sort of qualification, the would-be session musician would then seek to gain some experience with a regular band or orchestra. This would give the player experience of rehearsing and performing with other musicians under certain pressured conditions in the studio, on stage or both. This will give the player experience of playing with other musicians, under pressure, which will be invaluable when he or she decides to *go on the market* as a session musician.

There is also a new breed of session person, known as the *session programmer*, who is brought in to coordinate any sequencing, sampling or other computer technology which might be either required during a recording session or a live performance. Such talent is becoming increasingly important in the music business of the nineties, and people with such skills can command fees at least similar to those earned by a session musician.

WHAT IS A SESSION?

A recording session is quite simply the coming together of a number of musicians and singers for the purpose of recording a piece of music. That piece of music might be a single or an album track by a particular artist; it might be a *jingle* for a radio or television advertisement; or it might be all or part of the soundtrack for a film or television programme. Such pieces of music written and recorded for a particular event, product or purpose, are being recorded, day-in, day-out, the world over.

Most such sessions are staffed by *freelance* or *session* musicians because quite often such jobs are one-offs. It would be far too expensive for a studio, a film company, a rock singer or band to employ, say, a string section the whole year round. Far more economical is to identify exactly where and when you need strings on your album, your soundtrack or your jingle, and bring the string musicians, or *string section*, in for just that one job.

So where do we find these musicians? And how do we know they're the right musicians for the job? Answer: we don't necessarily, but the *fixer* does.

THE FIXER

Fixer is the somewhat inadequate term used to describe the person who seeks out, assembles and manages the group of musicians required for a session. Who employs the fixer, and indeed whether or not a fixer is used at all, depends very much on the type of session. If it's a rock session, then the producer, the artist's management and artist will have a say in the choice of fixer. If the session is more formal, for a film or television show, and without the *personality* of a recording by a name artist, then the producer in consultation with the arranger and possibly the composer will choose the fixer.

A fixer will have a very broad musical knowledge and background and some kind of formal musical training. He or she will need to have worked with many, many different musicians and will have a valuable address book full of names to suit every type of session.

Once contracted for a particular job, the fixer will find the musicians, draw up their contracts – a job which will include determining whether or not there will be royalties, a lump sum or both – ensure that all the musicians arrive at the right place at the right time, iron out any pre-session problems, stay there to see that all goes well and then that's it. Rarely does the fixer get involved in any post-session work; in fact, the only job left after the recording is over is to make sure agreed fees are paid. The fixer will receive a lump sum payment, which will include a fixing fee, and the rest will be distributed to the musicians, according to their contracts. And if the fixer's client fails to come up with the cash, it's still down to the fixer to pay the musicians.

So it is important that the session musician gets to know a network of fixers. The more fixers the session musician gets to know and gets on with, the more jobs will come his or her way.

There will, of course, be many jobs which don't involve a fixer; many producers (Chapter 8) carry a close-knit team of session players around with them and don't require the services of this middleman. To be a *favourite* of a top producer is any session player's dream as the respect that producer has within the industry will rub off on to the session players. As you can see, this section of the business is all about trust and contacts. A trustworthy, reliable session player who's in favour with a handful of trustworthy, reliable fixers and producers will always do well.

Fixers often form companies which both session musicians and producers will contact – for work and for services respectively. There are few of these companies in existence in the UK; many fixers work as sole operators, and their reputations spread by word of mouth. The names and addresses of fixers can be found in, among other places, the *Music Week Yearbook* (Appendix A).

THE SESSION: WHAT HAPPENS?

As studio time is expensive – costs include rental of space, equipment, engineers, catering and security staff, etc. – most people who are regularly involved in session work have it down to a fine art. In most cases a session will be structured so that a musician will be required for as short a time as possible. To have musicians hanging around waiting to play their part is costly and, while this sometimes cannot be avoided, the session will usually be organized so that each musician comes in and does his or her bit at the required time and then leaves. This may happen several days in a row, requiring the musician to commute backwards and forwards to a studio, but this is usually preferred by both the musician and the session organizers, and particularly by whoever is paying for the session!

If the budget permits, a session might well be taking place at one of the many luxurious studios which have been built in particularly attractive parts of the world. A top-selling, highly prized artist or producer might, for example, decide to record his or her next album in the Caribbean or in a chateau in the heart of the French countryside. And if session musicians are required, they too will have to be flown out to the said exotic location. Such sessions will cost a great deal of money because if a particular musician is only required for, say, 2 hours a day for 3 days, that musician will nonetheless have to be paid and fed and given accommodation on location for the full 3 days or more. Such jobs are every session musician's dream and they do come up once in a while. However, technology these days will allow many sessions to be recorded closer to home and mixed in later. It is by far the cheaper option and, as long as producer and artist were happy working with musicians in this remote way, that would be the way most people deal with this expensive problem.

In the studio

A musician has been booked for a session and the fee and working conditions have been agreed upon. The date of the session arrives and the musician turns up ready to work, in most cases, though not all, having had the sheet music for several days in order to be able to rehearse alone in advance of the session. Soundchecks will then be carried out, musicians will be positioned and miked up and then there will be a briefing from the fixer, producer, the singer, musician or band under whose name the music is being recorded, or the arranger (the person employed to write individual scores for each musician), or all of these. If this session is to be dubbed on to an existing track, the musicians will then have that backing track played and explained to them.

Then there will be a series of rehearsals, for individual instruments and for the whole ensemble. The session might, on the other hand, simply involve one instrument – a saxophone playing a solo over an instrumental break in a song and/or over the fade at the end. In such a case, the saxophonist will work through a series of ideas with all or some of the above, before the solo is attempted.

The take

Then comes the final *take*. This is hopefully what will be used on the finished recording and, ideally, it will work first time, in other words all musicians will play the right part to the right tempo to the satisfaction of all. This rarely happens, however, and most musicians will be prepared for several goes at a take.

If, for whatever reason, things just aren't working out, and the session *overruns*, things can now start to get costly. Many session musicians will have clauses in their contracts to deal with overruns; these will basically say that if the session goes over the agreed time, more money will be required. Overruns are to be avoided.

PAYMENT

The amount of money paid to a session musician varies according to the musician, the type of session and what happens to the music afterwards. Some musicians will have their own contract drawn up, which will include certain specific demands, although for all but the musician *in demand* there are fixed rules which have been established between the musicians' unions and the record industry.

For example, in the UK, a multitalented musician who is booked to play more than one part on a recording will be paid more for the second performance than for the first, and more for the third than for the second, and so on. This is a rule established by the Musicians' Union to encourage the use of as wide a variety of musicians as possible. The benefits of doubling up on musicians is debatable – you could say that overdubbing the same musician over and over again (however many different instruments he or she uses) might rob the sound of a certain texture. On the other hand, if you use the same multi-talented musician over and over again you're only having to deal with one person, and only one person has to learn the score.

The master

Sessions at which tracks are recorded for release as a single or as part of an album are usually referred to as *master sessions* and, given the number of rock and pop records released every week (often up to 100 new albums a week in the UK alone), it represents an important source of work for session musicians. Most session people will be paid a straight fee for playing on a master session, although here there is an opportunity for a top session musician to earn a royalty. Such a privilege is rarely afforded to a session musician, but there are those at the top of their profession who might even waive their set fee, or take a reduced set fee in return for *points* (or a percentage of royalties), particularly if it is certain that the record in question will be a big seller. Musicians will be paid for a master session, whether or not the recording is eventually released.

The demo

Demos or demonstration recordings provide regular work for a number of session musicians. These are often made for publishers interested in signing a particular writer who has not as yet had many or any songs recorded. Demos might be paid for by the publisher or by the artist's management and, if they are being done at the request of the A&R department of a record company, the company in question might pay. Session musicians might end up negotiating a slightly lower fee than that paid for a master session, simply because the demo recording is not intended for commercial exploitation. In some countries, an occasional bleep is recorded on to a demo so that it can't be used commercially without the permission of the various people involved in the session.

Film, television and radio

Payment structures for film and television vary from country to country. In the UK, for example, television companies pay repeat fees to session players for all music recorded for television except for signature tunes. Therefore, artists charge a higher rate for signature tune work. In the US, on the other hand, no television repeat fees are paid unless the programme is repeated on another medium – video or CD-I for example – and signature tunes are not regarded as any different from any other music recorded for television.

For live performance on television or radio, with a band or singer playing live on a music show for example, minimum rates are negotiated between the Musicians' Union and television companies, which vary in the case of television depending on whether or not the musician actually appears on camera. If a performance is repeated, all musicians receive a repeat fee. No single body monitors repeat performances; the Musicians' Union, which negotiated this payment structure on behalf of musicians, says that the repeat fees system works on trust. If a programme featuring live musical recordings is repeated, the television or radio executive responsible for the repeat broadcast will return to the original contract drawn up with the musicians concerned and they will be paid according to the contract. In the case of television programmes which after their original broadcast on a terrestrial channel are sold abroad or to satellite or cable channels, musicians again receive repeat fees, in accordance with *multimedia royalty agreements* between ITV and BBC and the Musicians' Union.

Session musicians will also receive a set fee for playing on a television commercial, which can be used for a certain number of times during a certain period (usually around 3 years), after which the musicians' original contracts would be renegotiated. Again, in the UK such renegotiation happens on trust, the Musicians' Union intervening only where a dispute arises.

In the case of jingles, such as those played by radio stations in between items or to identify a programme or presenter, musicians in the US will receive a low set fee and repeat fees (also known as *residuals*) every time the jingle is played. In the UK, musicians will usually receive only a set fee for jingles, unless the musician is also the writer and possibly even the producer, which is often the case. Then a US-type deal will be negotiated in which a lower set fee will be established in return for residuals.

Fees for music recorded for films, whether they're made for television or for theatrical release, will be negotiated on a job-by-job basis.

On stage

There are Musicians' Union minimums for live stage performances by session musicians, although these are of course open to abuse. In a classical situation, session musicians and singers will almost always get what's rightly theirs because live performance is often where most of the money is to be made in classical music, so musicians wouldn't accept or be able to survive on anything but the minimum.

In rock and pop, however, it is still the perceived view by many in the industry, and certainly by agents, managers and owners of live venues in the UK, that people ought to be grateful to be able to play live and so they rarely get what's due to them (Chapter 19).

In the case of a formal live performance, in an orchestra or a cabaret for example, set fees will be paid and an additional recording fee if the material performed is later used on an album or for broadcast.

BECOMING A SESSION PLAYER

To become a session player, you've got to play. You've got to play before breakfast, before dinner, before bedtime – through the night if necessary. You've got to be very good at your instrument, and this can only be achieved with practice. However instinctive a player you are, you will want some formal training, because session players will almost always stand a better chance of getting work if they can sight read.

A musical qualification would help too, and will be essential if you intend to become a session player in the classical field. If you do attend a musical academy, then several months before you qualify you should be putting yourself about. Speak to your teachers and ask them for every contact they feel might help you get work once you qualify. You might even consider forming your own band or singing group simply to gain experience.

Having gained experience which you could use to prove to a future employer that you're serious, your next step would be to record a demo tape. This can be done in your own or a friend's bedroom studio if the equipment is of a reasonable standard. You would otherwise be advised to save up and get a professional tape made, as the experience of being properly engineered would be valuable to you anyway.

Next, you will need to acquire a list of names and addresses of fixers, producers and arrangers. This could be obtained from other session musicians you might have got to know through college or from professional studios, which might make available a list of people.

These fixers, producers and arrangers must then be sent your tape, along with a professionally prepared CV indicating exactly your qualifications and any professional or semiprofessional experience you have had. They will then sit on your tape, and possibly never get back to you, unless you get back to them first. Keep on at them, get to know them, ask to sit in on sessions and prove you're both an easy person to get on with and keen to get into the business. It may take time before that call comes through from the fixer but there will always be a time when, at short notice, the fixer will need someone just like you, and that will be when you get your lucky break.

19

On the road

Unless you actually get around to doing it yourself, you will never believe the stories told to you about life on the road. Like the one about the three female fans found by a roadie in the back of the equipment truck with the bullwhip-wielding (male) manager of the club; or the one about the band jumping into a moving car in order to escape the club manager who wanted the band's blood after they justifiably criticized his venue while on stage; or the one about the club manager who when asked by the band, which had just played a trouble-free well-received two-hour set, for its meagre £25 payment told them to get out now (without it) if they wanted to get out alive; or the one about the band which was given a dressing room flooded by water from the neighbouring toilet and who therefore had to balance on the skirting boards of the room to stay dry while changing

The above represent a small proportion of true stories told by one young UK pop band trying to play to its reasonable-sized following when and wherever possible. This band almost always filled places wherever it played (thus earning valuable door money and bar takings for the venue), and neither its members nor fans ever caused any trouble.

This is not a sob story on behalf of the band, however, rather it is a sob story on behalf of the whole rock and pop music business. With the risk of tarring all venues with the same brush (and the authors apologize to those rare exceptions where young and upcoming bands are treated with respect), it is true to say that certainly in London and in most cities around the UK young unknowns will be treated badly by the management of most of the venues they play in the early days of touring. They will be paid a pittance too. Many won't be paid at all for that matter, and some will even be charged for the privilege of playing.

Upcoming rock and pop bands which play their own material should be prepared for the worst when embarking upon a life on the road; it will get better the more popular they become, but in the early days they'll suffer for their art.

SHOWS AND CABARET

Bad experiences will not apply so much to singers and bands who perform purely as a profession. The type of act discussed above is, by and large, aiming for dizzy heights, hoping to promote and profit from its (usually self-written) material and its intrinsic performing qualities. Venue managers know this and exploit such acts accordingly.

Showbands, those bands which often play known hits, either of a specific genre or era or simply faithfully reproduce current hits, are usually better treated and can afford to charge more because they are not in the business for anything more than the fee they're paid on the night. They are often employed as part of an evening of entertainment that might include a comedian, magician or solo singer.

The folk circuit is different, too, from that which the pop hopefuls have to suffer. Very much a semiprofessional circuit, there is not such a sense of urgency among the folk community and so nightly performances in clubs and pubs tend to be less pressured with less at stake. Managers see less to exploit and performers wouldn't put up with bad treatment because they're rarely aiming for the big time and therefore don't necessarily see every gig as a means to a star-studded end.

There is a whole other world of live music which never touches the mad and potentially money-spinning world of rock and roll, in which all manner of musicians and singers thrive, playing jazz, traditional music, ballroom dance music, big band music, classical chamber music and pretty well any other type of music you can think of on stage as performers in their own right or as part of a show.

Aspiring performers in these many and varied fields are

advised to get to know agents specializing in their particular type of music.

GETTING THE GIGS

In the early days, and we're talking specifically rock and pop here, this will be done by the artists themselves, and later by a manager (Chapter 4) or an agent (Chapter 13). If an act is paying a manager 15% and that manager in turn pays an agent 15% for securing the gig, it's worth noting that here the act will be paying twice for the privilege of getting a booking. In many cases these days managers bypass the agents and go straight to the venues. which will agree to allow an act to perform for one or more of the following reasons:

- The act, as demonstrated by demos, live recordings or word of mouth, is of the type that suits the venue. In other words, if the venue is famous for C&W then a competent sounding C&W act will stand a chance of getting a gig there.

- The act has a proven popular following in the venue's immediate locality.

- The act is becoming nationally known and/or has a current hit record.

- The act is approved by an agent which books regularly for the venue.

- The act has played a demo to the manager (or booker, the person who books in the entertainment) and that person simply likes what he or she has heard and wants to give the act a chance.

THE TOUR

Once a rock band has made it and is about to embark on its first national headlining tour it is simpler to look at the live music scene as a small industry in itself, employing a whole range of skilled people from HGV drivers to qualified electricians and from piano tuners to stage set builders and designers.

Take as an example the first night of a 30-date tour across the UK, with a band's second album showing signs of doing well across the country, but requiring promotion – hence the tour. The first album made the band's name, selling a surprising and very healthy 250 000 copies in the UK. There's a support band, too, paid for by the record company to which it recently signed.

The bands will be playing 1500- to 2500-seater venues, for which in the UK audiences are used to paying up to £18 a ticket. For this money they will, of course, expect the band to perform their hits, but they'll expect a little more besides. They will want the show to start on time (thus end on time to allow them to get trains, buses and taxis home); they will want good sound quality (they are all used to CDs at home now); they will want good lighting and stage design (videos and TV have set higher standards of presentation) and they will expect a clean, safe venue staffed by decent security people who will ensure their safety while at the same time leaving them free to enjoy the show unintimidated. A lot to ask? Some tour and venue managers might think so, but it is not really. You would pay the same (and you would have the chance of paying less) in a West End theatre and there you would expect exactly this standard, if not a better standard, of presentation. So let's look at all those audience expectations stage by stage, and consider the work and the personnel required to ensure that those expectations are met.

The performance

The performance itself is the direct responsibility of the act. Whether it is a band of singer–songwriters or a solo singer–songwriter, most of the decisions concerning what will be played when and how will be made by the people who wrote, played and sang the top-selling songs in the first place. Some bands will always have been able to handle this themselves; others will require a musical director or producer, such as they used in the studio. This person will cost money, and will usually be found by the A&R person or the manager or both, in collaboration with the band.

The biggest problem facing any band with a hit album or two under its belt is to get the live sound to match the recorded sound. Of course, no audience wants to hear a record reproduced up there on stage, but the excitement of hearing a recording you know and love played out in front of you on stage is part of what going to hear a modern live concert is all about.

Only certain types of act can get away with not doing so, either by rearranging the hits or by not playing them at all, but such a perverse approach to live playing rarely works. Elvis Costello often does this to varying degrees and usually gets away with it. Elton John, on the other hand, once played both sides of a brand new unheard album (*Captain Fantastic And The Brown Dirt Cowboy*) at an all-star summer stadium show in London and bombed! The album is today hailed as a classic, but what fan could make that sort of assessment while listening under sweltering sun surrounded by a 60 000-strong crowd there to hear hits, more hits and nothing but the hits?

So, a set list of songs is planned and rehearsals are under way. Meanwhile, the stage set and lighting have to be designed.

The designer and production manager

Flamboyant stage sets are less common today than they were in the seventies and early eighties when giant blow-up pigs, sheep and male genitalia, crashing aeroplanes, cranes, cannons, trapezes and the like were the order of the day. Such over-the-top sets are still used, particularly by heavy rock acts, but increasingly in the nineties bands go for the clear, empty stage which is allowed by the increasingly compact nature of so much of the technology used today.

However subtle the design, whether it reflects the design of an album cover or the styling in a particularly popular video, a designer will be brought in at this stage to discuss ideas and talk them through with the production manager to ensure that the ideas are feasible logistically.

The production manager is hired on a tour-by-tour basis (bands, managers and A&R people will have their favourites, but will ultimately be answerable to the promoter) to run the technical side of things. The production manager will contract all the technical services required, such as sound, lighting, transport, rigging and catering, and will coordinate their activities throughout the tour, hence the production manager's input into the stage design. Looking at the whole tour in logistical terms, the production manager is in a strong position to say of the design ideas 'that will work, but that won't'.

The production manager is very often a sole operator, in other words self-employed: known in the business and simply called upon, when needed, by a promoter who knows and trusts the person in question. A good production manager working in this way will most likely manage to get work through word-of-mouth recommendation and may well be able to operate with little more than a phone and address book. Once the tour has been budgeted (which the production manager will have a say in) he or she will then set about finding the equipment and personnel to suit the particular tour in question.

Some big promoters will employ a production manager full time.

 ## Starting on time

The tour has been booked by the promoter (Chapter 13) and all the right deals have been struck with the various venue managements. So now to the logistics, which are the responsibility of the *tour manager*, who is brought in by the band's manage- ment (sometimes, but not always, at the recommendation of the promoter) to ensure that all the elements which come under the jurisdiction of the band, its manager and the production manager fit properly into the scheme of things. The tour manager will work with the transport and travel people to ensure that everyone reaches the right place at the right time. If this does not happen, the show will not start on time.

Like production managers, tour managers might be sole operators or may be permanently employed by a big artist's management company, or might even be proprietors of their own tour management company. What is to distinguish between the tour manager and the production manager? The former manages the band on the road while the latter manages the staging of the show. Even on a world tour, the tour manager will travel for its duration, coordinating press, TV and radio interviews for the band, ensuring that travel arrangements go smoothly and so on. The production manager is less likely to be involved in the tour on an ongoing basis. He or she will plan the logistics of the actual show and perhaps tour with the entourage in the home country; however, when the tour leaves for another country, it is likely than the promoter for that country will have allocated a local production manager to that particular leg of the tour.

So, once the production manager knows what's required

technically, and once the band and its management are clear what will happen artistically, key personnel – band, band management, promoter, production manager and tour manager – will meet to finalize plans.

ON THE NIGHT

As the audience walk through the turnstiles, get their tickets clipped, grab a beer and a hot dog and then settle in their seats in anticipation of a (hopefully) great night's entertainment, it is unlikely that the work required to bring the show even to this stage ever passes through most of their minds.

Yet work in the theatre probably began at around 8 a.m. And if this were a major, stadium-sized tour, it's quite likely that there would be a replica stage set with replica crew setting up already for the same gig 2 days ahead somewhere else in the country and possibly somewhere else in the world.

 So, at 8 a.m., the *riggers* are at work. These are the people who hang cables, erect lighting towers and other forms of scaffolding where required, and essentially build into the venue any of the hardware that is not already there.

 While this is going on, the *roadies* will be unloading the lighting and sound equipment and stage set. Often a proportion of this *road crew* will be hired locally to work on a certain stretch of the tour only. Local crews are most frequently used on world tours, when it proves too costly to fly all the required personnel from base to host country.

 Coordinated by the production manager, roadies, riggers and any specialists, for example forklift operators, electricians, joiners and audiovisual technicians required to coordinate special video and laser effects, etc., will work around each other through the day to a point at around 4.30 p.m. when all will be ready for the headline band's soundcheck. Inevitably, not everything will be ready by then, but the soundcheck time will certainly be stipulated in the band's *rider* (Chapter 13), and if the soundcheck isn't allowed to happen the promoter will be the person who is ultimately responsible.

The headline band's soundcheck complete, if there's any time left the support band will get a soundcheck. The support band's soundcheck is, however, often the subject of great controversy. Usually the headline act's contract will specify that no support band equipment will be set up until the headline act's equipment is up and tested, that under no circumstances must the support band touch or interfere with the headliner's equipment in any way and that if the headliner's soundcheck overruns into the support band's soundcheck time, basically, tough luck!

For as long as anyone can remember support bands and their management have cried foul in such circumstances, claiming that the headliners have deliberately denied the support act a soundcheck to ensure that they, the headliners, sound technically better on the night. Can we say there is some truth in this? Yes, we can.

The very fact that headline acts have been known deliberately to cheat the support act out of a soundcheck proves how important the soundcheck is. Soundchecks are all about balance and tone. If a bass guitar drowns out a lead guitar or the drums drown out the vocals, an act's performance and material will suffer. A soundcheck beforehand, with people in the auditorium listening and guiding the performers on how volume levels and so on should be set, can ensure that a group of musicians and singers will be able to go on stage without having to wonder whether or not they will sound all right to the audience. Fiddling with amplifiers, mixing desks and microphones during a set can kill it dead. To any group of performers that cares about how it sounds, a soundcheck is essential.

THE JOBS ON THE ROAD

Rock and roll tours offer employment to a wide range of skilled people, from electricians to drivers, from computer programmers to instrument tuners and from caterers to stage set builders. Few such people will be employed permanently by anyone directly connected with the music business.

Production and tour managers might have started out as roadies or in some other area of showbusiness in which they acquired the skills required to coordinate a tour. The tour manager might well have started out in some area of the travel business, while the production manager might have had experience as a theatre stage manager or as a roadie with a particular specialist skill.

Road crew members, or roadies, may simply be good at lifting things, getting up on time and being fun to be with on tour or they might have a useful ancillary skill such as those of electrician or sound engineer; they will often be employed purely on a freelance basis. They will get to know certain bands or artist management companies, or they may be on the books of certain production managers or transportation companies. Their work will usually come through a phone call at home. 'Can you do so and so's tour for 6 months starting in 8 weeks' time?' Money will be fought over and contracts will be signed, and if the roadie does a good job, word will get around and work will most likely come the roadie's way on a fairly regular basis.

Tour caterering staff will usually be employed by catering firms which specialize in such work. Promoters, tour and production managers will have their favourites, and so will the artists. The same goes for the transportation companies. There are firms which specialize in moving stage and theatre equipment around (they are often the same firms which hire out the equipment); and there are also firms which specialize in moving people around – by private jet if the tour goes worldwide and the act is well known and a high earner or by coaches (kitted out in varying degrees of luxury) if the tour is fairly local or is going to places not well served by airports.

GETTING ON TO A TOUR

You won't get on to a tour without a track record or a recommendation. Often, an interest in music or musical knowledge will not necessarily count in your favour. If you apply to a catering firm which specializes in rock and roll tours and all you talk about in your interview is how you'd love to go on tour with a rock band, you might give the impression that your heart is not in the cooking!

The same goes for the road crew, the drivers, the riggers and pretty well everyone else involved. The road is no place for the star struck. In the case of some roadies, the ability to play, tune and maintain a guitar, a piano or some other instrument will help because as a band gets bigger (in terms of success) so each member might wish or need to have his or her own roadie to look after and tune his or her set of instruments.

Clearly the sound crew (which may come with the hired sound equipment) will need technical and musical skills, experience and even qualifications, but in all cases the ability to get on with people under pressure, often in most unpleasant places and conditions, counts as much as anything else you have to offer.

Before deciding upon a life on the road, you will want to have thought long and hard about what it does to your health, your personal relationships and your sanity. It's a false life in many ways and the sensitive rarely survive it. You may have read and heard stories about how it's all one big party and that sex, drugs and drink flow freely and, somehow, everyone survives. That isn't altogether true. It can be said that, in these artificial circumstances, people do behave in a way that they might not at home, sometimes because the opportunity presents itself and sometimes simply as a way of surviving the loneliness and the pressure which goes with the job. Much riotous after-show behaviour is down to the adrenaline rush that comes with working in this business. The show's over, it's bedtime but you're pumped up with this natural drug and you need to do something to accommodate the feeling it gives you. Here is where the trouble can start.

Many of the stories you hear are exaggerated, however, and it can be a shock to find a road crew or a band sitting quietly in the hotel after a gig drinking tea and reading the newspaper. Some will be disappointed to find that in many cases such behaviour is the norm.

The main point to remember is that as touring is all about a diverse bunch of people living together in strange places and working long hours at the wrong times of the day, there are few generalizations that can be made about it. You will have to research carefully the jobs you consider and take any job step by step once you get it. And if you're looking for a job for life with a good pension, holidays and a regular growing income, then a life 'on the road' is not for you.

20

The star

Is stardom really what all would-be singers, singer–songwriters and musicians are aiming at? There are some who will be driven from the start to make it to the very top and, if they drive themselves hard, are totally single-minded in their goal and pursue it to the exclusion of all else (and of course have the talent to justify such means to an end), they stand a fair chance of achieving it.

Few people are like that, however. Few are able to sustain the level of determination required to *make it*. Few are able to ignore the distractions of family and other relationships, and those who do (and to become a big star you have to) usually leave trails of hurt people in their wake. And few have the single-minded approach which allows them to forge ahead in their ambitions while others within the music business, and some outside it, serve to hamper their efforts, intentionally or otherwise. Whatever it is that drives a would-be star upwards, it has the power to upset lives and careers along the way. That may sound overdramatic, but few who have reached the dizzy heights would disagree. The route to the top is long and painful, both for the stars and for the people around them.

Here we're talking about the very top. It is important to remember that sustained stardom (such as that enjoyed by the likes of Elton John, The Rolling Stones, Bob Dylan, Bruce Springsteen, Paul Simon, Paul McCartney, Eric Clapton and U2 – in the field of music almost exclusive to the rock and pop world) is so rare that it is impossible to make generalizations about, and impossible to hold up one example as a model.

WHAT IS STARDOM?

Stardom is not part of a natural progression. You don't automatically become a star once you reach a certain level of record sales and, conversely, you don't necessarily cease to be a star once your record sales start to fall.

British band Supertramp, formed in 1969, is a perfect example of success without stardom. Their succession of hit albums released between 1974 and 1984 together sold millions of copies the world over, spawning hit singles which are still played on the radio today. Yet if you bumped into Richard Davies in the street you would never know him as the person who created their distinctive keyboard sound and who sang lead vocals on such hits as Breakfast In America, It's Raining Again and The Logical Song.

Supertramp once spoke of the dubious privilege they used to enjoy of being able to walk, unrecognized, up and down the aisles of the 10 000-seater auditoriums they used to play, as their audience was filing in. By contrast, Bob Geldof at the massive Irish charity concert Self Aid, held in Dublin in 1986, had to leave his seat in the VIP box during a performance by the band Clannad because the audience, who had spotted Geldof, had turned to cheer him and was both ignoring and drowning out the band on stage.

So stardom isn't always about record sales. The multimillion album sales enjoyed by Supertramp didn't guarantee stardom and, conversely, Geldof was enjoying adoration of biblical proportions at a time when his record sales were most definitely nothing to cheer about.

LEVELS OF STARDOM

As stardom and levels of success become easier to exploit the more sophisticated the industry becomes, so a *science of stardom* is emerging. For example, there are *A-lists* and *B-lists*. There are even *C-lists* and *D-lists*. These lists exist in the record company executives' minds, in the promoters' minds (Chapter 13) and in the minds of those people working in music television, particularly those involved in the huge concerts which are televised the world over. They indicate levels of stardom which are translated into audience sizes – concert and TV audiences. A line-up of A-list people (all those listed above are A-list) will guarantee a television audience of global proportions, as did *Live Aid*, the *Human Rights Now* concert tour and the *Mandela Day* event, while a bill made up primarily of B-list acts will guarantee a sizeable live audience but television distribution limited to certain territories, depending upon the artists involved, and so on.

It is unlikely, though, that any artists would want to stand up and grade themselves A, B or C. Modesty, the fear of tempting fate or sheer ignorance of such detail would prevent most from doing so. However, in the minds of the television executives, the concert promoters and the record company bosses, such classifications are important, and increasingly so as the multinational music business becomes more about corporate identity, size and power and less about singers, songwriters, their music and their fans.

Stars, the majors and the law

Every major multinational record label (Chapter 4) wants its A-list artist, a couple if possible. That's why A-list artists are paid such ridiculously high sums to sign (or re-sign) with these companies. The A-listers act as a sort of flagship for such companies, a mascot, something to please the shareholders, something to wave in the face of the competition.

The stakes are high in this game. What sort of image does it give your company when you suddenly find that the deals you have with your two highest profile A-list artists start to look shaky – as has happened to Sony with its flagship signings George Michael and Michael Jackson? Did the artists concerned ever dream that this is what it would be like at the top? Did front-page headlines about multimillion-dollar deals and sex-scandals figure in the original game plan? Where do the fans and a love of music fit in to such a scenario?

Again, we must bring things back into perspective. This is not the average rock star's career. To the many thousands of people who decide to have a go at making a career in music, such events are irrelevant now and always will be.

Let's consider for a moment three generations of British megastars starting with The Beatles, who made it big in the early sixties, Elton John, who made it big in the early seventies, and George Michael, who made it big in the early eighties. Give or take a year or two, all three found themselves involved in prolonged, headline-making court cases within a decade of getting to the top. And there was nothing glamorous about those court cases; they weren't about driving sports cars into swimming pools, throwing televisions out of hotel windows or being caught with the spouse of a top politician. No, they were about business. And in all three cases the artists were fighting people who had been instrumental in their success.

So success at its highest level is rarely without its problems. The early successes enjoyed by aspiring artists, too, can be marred by unforeseen forces, such as panic, lack of direction and an overzealous media.

EARLY SUCCESSES

Rock and pop recording artists are increasingly living out the anxieties and the pressures of success in public these days, often through no fault of their own. The media may have a lot to answer for. There hasn't been a Beatles-type phenomenon since The Beatles, yet since that band's arrival in the early sixties so much of popular music's commentators' time has been divided between trying to find *the next Beatles* and speculating over when or whether the band would get back together again. This speculation continues even now there are only three members alive today, which goes to show how increasingly difficult it must be to find an interesting rock/pop subject to write or talk about. While The Beatles continue to disappoint the showbusiness journalists by not reforming, journalists spend their time speculating on how big, or how Beatles-like, the next upcoming stars are going to get.

Hype

So, a band like eighties UK success story The Smiths, for example, shows originality, acquires a large cult following, and the press go berserk. Article after article is written about the band's impact on British pop culture and, years after the band disbands, the articles continue.

The Smiths weren't as big as The Beatles, The Rolling Stones, The Police or U2; nothing like as big. But they were innovative, certainly different enough to give the rock and pop pundits something to enthuse about. The trouble is that, in such a situation, such a band gets little opportunity to develop out of the public eye.

An early nineties sensation, the US band Nirvana, surprised many when its second album, *Nevermind*, sold over seven million copies worldwide. Its commercial success notwithstanding, Nirvana also proved to be a media dream come true. The band was credited with spearheading the *grunge* movement (typified by rugged guitar playing and a hair-in-the-face attitude) which gave journalists and DJs the perfect peg to hang them on, and its front man, the late lamented Kurt Cobain, and his widow Courtney Love had a lovely long list of headline-worthy personal problems on which to draw.

So, while the more sensational media coverage focused on the turbulent life of the troubled Kurt Cobain, the more heavyweight commentators could spend time speculating over whether the follow-up album to *Nevermind*, *In Vitro*, would (a) ever get made and (b) be as good as the first. The build up to and hype surrounding the follow-up to a hit album can, arguably, damage its chances before it ever hits the streets. It can certainly affect the artists' approach to the creation of the second album, and it can certainly affect the marketing strategy. Suddenly a band or a singer–songwriter finds itself/him or herself writing and recording an album taking place under a completely different set of conditions from those which prevailed when the first one was made.

The first album often has a whole lifetime of experiences woven into it, and is in many ways the tangible evidence of a goal achieved in spite of very difficult circumstances. The second, on the other hand, is made often under the media spotlight. If the first was a hit there is that to consider when making the second; and if the media adored the first, *will the second be as good as the first* ? Speculative stories can often provide sufficient hype to ensure that the follow-up will, without doubt, be an anticlimax.

We are not suggesting that hard-core fans will ever be swayed away from their idols by the media. If a hard-core fan base is not given time to build, then it is the floating voters as represented by the media who will be determining the fate of our young stars, and we know how fickle they can be.

Manufactured stardom

The prevailing economic climate worldwide and the short-termism that it has fostered in many sectors of industry (if it's not making a profit, close it down) have seeped into the music business to the point at which bands are rarely signed for multi-album deals any longer. This means that if one or two albums fail, the record company can dump a band fast without too great a financial loss. The band might get picked up by an indie with a clearer idea of the band's potential, but often the time delay that such a transition causes can be enough to kill a band forever.

This is the danger of instant stardom, and today instant stardom is built into the music business. Some record companies are built around the concept, the hugely successful Stock, Aitken and Waterman organization for example, which in the eighties chewed up and spat out such a large number of teen disco stars from all walks of life, most of whom few of us could name today. The company made millions along the way, and the chances are that most of its artists were aware of the likely short-term nature of their stardom. To hold Stock, Aitken and Waterman up as an example of how stardom and success can be manufactured (but as such must be short-lived) is not to judge or to criticize but simply to illustrate how the nature of success has changed since rock and pop created its first world superstars. Can you name the next Elton John, Prince, Guns'n'Roses or Nirvana? You probably cannot.

STARDOM: THE PERSONAL ANGLE

Is everything we read in the papers true? Do all the big names in the music business inevitably succumb to the temptations of drink, drugs, extramarital affairs and all the other vices which we are led to believe is the stuff of stardom? The answer to that question is no; or, at least, it is not as simple as that. Firstly, it is not just the people at the top of the music business who have found it hard to resist such temptations. In the pre-recession economic boom of the eighties, when there was an attempt by certain sectors of the press to make celebrities of the city slickers or so-called *yuppies* who were making vast sums of money at that time, it became clear that certain people at the top of that tree were falling prey to the trappings of high-profile success: cocaine, champagne and a totally artificial, 24 hours a day lifestyle which can cause family and other loved ones to take second place, temporarily at least.

It is not just rock stars who take drugs and have affairs. One can generalize by saying that to make it to the top in the music business requires total single-mindedness because there are so many forces such as fashion, the press, rivalry and personal life which, intentionally or otherwise, work against the aspiring rock or pop hero. This single-mindedness manifests itself in a number of ways, depending upon the person. If the would-be star is to succeed, he or she must ignore all distractions until success has been won.

Can you name one rock star (other than Paul McCartney!) whose first marriage is still intact? It is the first marriages which usually suffer from the rock and roll way of life, partly because in those early days when the fight to get to the top is on there's never enough time to attend to the marriage. Also, stardom (success, drugs, money, fame and adoration) can change people so that the person who made the marriage vows before rising to the top is a different person once success has been achieved.

Does all this mean, therefore, that if you're determined to make it to the top as a performer in the music business you will suffer either personal relationship problems, a drink or drugs problem, or all of these and more? The answer is probably yes. That's the price you pay for such a high level of wealth and success. Most important to remember is that a fraction of 1% of the people aiming for stardom in this business at any given time ever achieve it. And if that last statement leads you to believe that you might therefore not make it to the top, then you won't! There is no room for self-doubt at the top of the rock and roll tree.

MEDIUM-SIZED SUCCESS

Most performers in the music business are not megastars, and are happy that way. Sustained megastardom requires such extraordinary drive, talent and personality that is and always will be a rarity in the business. Overnight stardom that goes as quickly as it comes can be manufactured but probably isn't what most people are seeking, while a sustained level of success and a manageable level of fame sounds ideal.

The latter situation is also enjoyed by comparatively few acts as it relies on a consistent standard of songwriting and performance, durability of material and style in the face of rapidly changing trends, and a record company that is prepared to stick with the act in question in spite of the fact that profits will always be comparatively modest.

The changing structure of the music business, which frequently involves mergers and takeovers and therefore personnel changes at the top, means that such acts can lose record company support suddenly and at a stroke. A change in a record company's management structure can mean that, suddenly, a particular artist or band doesn't fit into the scheme of things. If, for example, their profits fluctuate too greatly (something which might have been tolerated by previous management) or if the record company *repositions* itself to fit into other emerging trends in the business, then they lose out.

Even the highly acclaimed, low-key, long-serving stars of the music business, such as Elvis Costello and Squeeze in the UK are rarities and becoming increasingly so these days. What keeps the aforementioned going, in fact, is their prolific writing skills coupled with their commitment to making live appearances. Stop playing live at this level in particular, and you're history.

WHEN THE BUBBLE BURSTS

Whatever *did* happen to so and so? It's the saddest of questions and so frequently asked. Very often, the people you thought were so promising and from whom you expected years of service dropped out of the public eye and ear for political reasons: the band wasn't getting on or there were legal problems and, by the time they were sorted out, it was too late. Rarely do singer–songwriters or bands simply lose their talent – their ability to write or play. The sudden fall from the top can be down to the fact that the act should never have been at the top in the first place – that it was hyped there and the hype couldn't last or that it rode there on the back of some trend or other – but usually the circumstances which see an act sink into obscurity are complex, messy and unfortunate.

So what happens afterwards? How easy is it for members of a

band which has lost its popularity to pick up the pieces and form new bands or embark upon solo careers? The fate of the ex-members of a defunct band often depends on where the songwriting talent came from in the first place, and the reasons why the band split or lost public favour.

As a rule, the people who have enjoyed solo success after having been in a successful band are usually those whose talent or ambition (or both) has naturally outgrown and even over-shadowed the band which brought them fame in the first place – people for whom the band eventually became little more than a support system for their talent. The careers of Sting, Michael Jackson, Prince and George Michael serve to illustrate this point. Those who are forced to find new outlets for their talents as a result of a band splitting (or its front man or woman leaving to go solo) tend to do less well. The other half of Wham!, Andrew Ridgeley, Tony Hadley of UK new romantic band Spandau Ballet, Bruce Foxton and Rick Buckler of popular UK mod combo The Jam, and even the remaining Jacksons, are among many such cases. It is unlikely that the remaining members of UK band Queen and US band Nirvana will ever again achieve the levels of success they previously enjoyed before the tragic deaths of their front men.

THE ALTERNATIVES

Many who have tasted a year or two of stardom but then lose it move behind the scenes, into production, A&R or management. And then there are those who become butchers, bakers and candlestick makers.

Few who do leave the limelight are bitter about it, unless the fall from fame came about through the malice or incompetence of others. It is never easy to blame someone else totally, how-ever, for in rock and roll, as with other areas of life, whatever other forces are at work, it is you who ultimately makes the decisions about what you do and what you do not do.

21

The summing up

Julian Newby

If you expected to come away from this book with a clear idea of the qualifications and CV required for the particular music business job you are looking for, we apologize.

The important message is that there are no clear paths into any areas of the business. Career advice from Maurice Oberstein, a man who has been at the top of the business in the UK for many years, notably as the chairman of CBS Records, the chairman of PolyGram Records and chairman of the British Phonographic Industry, reads as follows:

> My advice is do not be too particular about your first job. I believe that in general we are quick to spot talented people and move them to jobs where they can contribute. Try all avenues of getting started, and be prepared to do a hum-drum job at the beginning. Successful people in the music business learn fast and take their opportunities.

> Develop your skills as widely as possible. The pop music business is still a young people's business: successful people get promoted quickly and suddenly find themselves operating at a much higher and wider level than ever before and using new skills.

Oberstein concludes:

> You will need one common quality for success, total commitment. It is not a business for the lukewarm or faint-hearted approach.

Most people in the music business would agree with Oberstein's observations. Otherwise, there are few other generalizations that can be made about the music business, although we can add one certainty, and that is that it is a very fickle and fast-changing business.

Increasingly, artists are enjoying success one minute and disappearing from the scene the next; record companies are shying away from big money contracts; back-catalogue is growing in importance as record companies discover new methods and formats with which to exploit existing material; big companies are swallowing the smaller ones; *hardware* and *software* are increasingly coming together under one roof; vinyl is becoming a rarity, and the CD is going interactive.

But these are not tales of doom and gloom; this all simply serves to demonstrate that the artist is just the tip of the iceberg in the music business, below which there are hundreds and thousands of people working day-in and day-out to find, promote and sustain new acts. Sometimes those new acts work; many more times they do not. But, clearly, the ones that do succeed bring in sufficient revenue to allow the others at least to have a go.

What is more, these artists are playing to an audience of record and CD buyers and concert goers which is becoming increasingly fickle by the day. The development of low-cost computer technology which has allowed the mass marketing of domestic computer hardware has presented the modern record industry with its first serious competitor ever: the computer game. The music business had it easy for too long; magazines and television programmes would provide the necessary publicity, showing videos, publishing pin-ups, song lyrics, personality profiles and the like – creating and maintaining the artists' star status – while the record companies pumped singles, tapes, albums and CDs into the shops to satisfy the demands of the world's star-struck youth.

Then along came computer games and sell-through videos, and suddenly young people began to ask themselves: what offers more value for money: a £3 single which lasts 3 minutes, which I might play 10 times, and which will show up on a compilation in a few weeks anyway; a £12 CD which lasts 45 minutes and which I might tire of after two or three plays; a £30 computer game which can last an infinite amount of time and which I can play over and over again, with friends or without; or a £14 movie which lasts 90 minutes, which I might watch five times, maybe more, and which I can record over once I'm bored with it?

And if all that's not enough of a challenge to the established record industry, further developments in digital technology have plunged the industry into a dilemma over *how* we're going to be listening to its music in the years to come. A digital tape format, the DCC, has been developed to replace the compact cassette (it's the same shape and size) and which offers CD-quality music plus text facilities; a recordable mini-CD or mini-disc has also been developed, posing a direct challenge to DCC as the next mass-market portable sound carrier; and, meanwhile, CD-I (that's interactive CD with pictures, readable only on a special CD-I machine) and CD-ROM (that's interactive CD with pictures, readable only on a PC with CD-ROM drive) are now threatening to become mass market and are each able to offer music, computer games, movies and much more – all from one machine.

What's more, digital radio stations, which come into our homes in the same way that cable TV does, are currently in development (and some are up and running) and will offer 30, 40 or more themed channels of CD-quality music. With all this and domestic digital recording facilities, who needs to go out and buy a CD?

Possibly nobody does, because mail-order record retailing is also a growth business. Just pick up the phone, name the CD or CDs of your choice, give your credit card number, and the discs will be with you in a matter of days. Now your friendly local record store no longer exists, this could provide the perfect alternative to a bus ride to the nearest big town for a visit to the megastore which might not stock the record you're looking for because it's not a big seller that month.

So is it really all change for the music business? Well, it has always been all change for the music business, if you think about it.

When The Beatles recorded Love Me Do, the compact cassette didn't exist and neither did the personal stereo. When they made *Sergeant Pepper's Lonely Heart's Club Band*, there were no 48-track studios. There were no eight-track studios for that matter. That album was done using four-track technology. Today, there's no limit to the number of tracks available to the studio artist.

The eight-track cartridge has come and gone; the laser disc has as good as come and gone and the Betamax video cassette and player have come and gone. The vinyl album was all but dead by the start of this decade and as we reach the middle of this decade the singles charts will have drastically reduced in importance.

Recordings can now be made, and regularly are, using no traditional instruments and no tape. Computers replace the instruments and computer disks replace the tape.

Computers cannot discover talent though, and they cannot write songs. They can't organize tours, they can't produce recordings and they can't sing very well on stage. And if there is a proliferation of digital radio stations and if we do start buying records over the phone rather than by visiting a record store (it's not as much fun browsing through CD cases as it was browsing through 12" album sleeves, after all) then we are still going to need people to make those records, which means we will need the A&R people to find the talent, the producers to shape the recordings, the managers to organize the artists and the lawyers to draw up the contracts between managers and record companies, which we'll also still need to make certain that the records keep being made.

So yes, the music business is changing, but do not let the idea that a changed music business means a diminished music business or a music business that's not as good or as fun as it was in the eighties, seventies or sixties. At various times during all three decades, there have been those who have preached that *the end of the music business is nigh.*

But the fact is, the end isn't nigh. The end of vinyl is nigh: some say it's here. Wax 78s died at the end of the fifties but that didn't kill off the industry. Singles might be on their way out, although songs will always be used to promote albums, and the compact cassette is most definitely out-of-date technology. Something will replace it though.

The evidence is that all these changes – in the corporate ownership of record companies, in methods of playing and recording, in the way in which music is delivered to our homes and even to our ears – have totally failed to put a stop to the never-ending supply of youthful enthusiasm which brings musicians, singers and songwriters together in the pursuit of the perfect song, regardless of whether or not that song is going to earn them or anyone else any money.

Throughout the UK, and throughout the world at this moment, young people are scraping together the cash for instruments in order that they might realize their dream of forming a band; young and old are playing for peanuts in clubs and even on street corners just for the pleasure of it, and songwriters are sitting with pen, paper and their chosen instrument, writing words and music which may or may not be heard by more than a handful of people, let alone earn anyone any money.

As has been said several times, the music business is about making money from copyright compositions. While all this activity continues, there will always be new compositions, which means that, whatever it looks like, whoever owns what company and however the music eventually reaches our homes and our ears, there will always be a music business.

Appendix A

Music industry addresses

COLLECTING/LICENSING ORGANIZATIONS

Educational Recording Agency (ERA)
33–34 Alfred Place
London WC1 7DP
Tel: 0171 436 4883
Fax: 0171 323 0486

Issues licences to educational establishments and authorities to record broadcast programmes for educational purposes.

Mechanical Copyright Protection Society Ltd (MCPS)
Elgar House
41 Streatham High Road
Streatham
London SW16 1ER
Tel: 0181 769 4400
Fax: 0181 769 8792

Collects 'mechanical' royalties due to publisher and composer from the recordings of their copyright musical works. The MCPS issues licences to the producers of CDs, records, tapes, videos, audiovisual, broadcast and film productions.

Performing Rights Society (PRS)
29–33 Berners Street
London W1P 4AA
Tel: 0171 580 5544
Fax: 0171 631 4138

Collects and distributes worldwide performance royalties on behalf of composer and publisher members. Derives income from the control of broadcasting and performing rights. The PRS issues licences to all kinds of venues and TV and radio broadcasters. Contact PRS for the telephone numbers and addresses of its regional offices.

Phonographic Performance Ltd (PPL)
Ganton House
14–22 Ganton Street
London W1V 1LB
Tel: 0171 437 0311
Fax: 0171 437 0311

PPL is a non-profit-making organization established in 1934 by the recording industry to administer the public performance and broadcasting rights of recordings. PPL issues licences to all kinds of venues and radio and TV broadcasters. Video Performance Limited (VPL) can be contacted at the same address.

US COLLECTING SOCIETIES

ASCAP
7920 Sunset Boulevard
Suite 300
Los Angeles
CA 90046
Tel: 00 1 213 883 1000
Fax: 00 1 213 883 1049

ASCAP (UK address)
Suite 10/11
52 Haymarket
London SW1Y 4RP
Tel: 0171 973 0069
Fax: 0171 973 0068

BMI
320 West 57th Street
New York
NY 10019
Tel: 00 1 212 586 2000
Fax: 00 1 212 245 8986

BMI (UK address)
79 Harley House
Marylebone Road
London NW1 5HN
Tel: 0171 935 8517
Fax: 0171 487 5091

SONGWRITER/COMPOSER/MUSICIAN/PUBLISHER
ORGANIZATIONS

Black Music Industry Association (BMIA)
146 Manor Park Road
London NW10
Tel: 0181 961 4857
Fax: 0181 453 0428

Advises and supports musicians, composers, publishers and record companies on all aspects relating to the industry. The BMA is not an association exclusively for black people. It is set up for anyone involved in the production, performance and promotion of black music.

British Academy of Songwriters, Composers and Authors (BASCA)
34 Hanway Street
London W1P 9DE
Tel: 0171 436 2261
Fax: 0171 436 1913

An organization of popular songwriters who are PRS members. BASCA can offer a wide range of general advice to its members. The Association of Professional Composers (APC) and the Composers' Guild of Great Britain (CGGB) can be contacted at the same address. Telephone APC on 0171 436 0919 and CGGB on 0171 436 0007.

Independent Publishers' Association
PO Box 3163
London NW1 5HH
Tel: 0171 935 8517
Fax: 0171 487 5091

Represents and offers support and advice to smaller, independent publishing companies.

The Musicians' Union (MU)
60–62 Clapham Road
London SW9 0JJ
Tel: 0171 582 5566
Fax: 0171 582 9805

Seeks to improve the status and remuneration of its members by protecting both contractual and statutory rights. Establishes pay agreements covering every type of employment for musicians, and also makes representations to parliament on a wide range of music-related issues. Contact the MU for the telephone numbers of its regional offices.

Music Publishers' Association (MPA)
3rd Floor
Strandgate
18/20 York Buildings
London WC2N 6JU
Tel: 0171 839 7779
Fax: 0171 839 7776

An organization of UK music publishers promoting and protecting their mutual interests, providing information for good publishing practice. Owns and supports MCPS Ltd.

INDUSTRY ORGANIZATIONS

Association of Professional Recording Services Ltd (APRS)
2 Windsor Square
Silver Street
Reading RG1 2TH
Tel: 01734 756218
Fax: 01734 756216

Promotes the interests of those involved with professional sound recording.

British Association of Record Dealers (BARD)
Kingsland House
514 Wimbourne Road East
Ferndown BH22 9NG
Tel: 01202 896395
Fax: 01202 895601

Acts as a forum for all music retailers within the UK. Protects the interests of its members in all matters that concern them, e.g. law, packaging, new technology and distribution.

British Phonographic Industry (BPI)
25 Savile Row
London W1X 1AA
Tel: 0171 287 4422
Fax: 0171 287 2252
Anti-piracy hotline: 0171 437 1493

Represents the UK record industry to government, Brussels and the general public, also liaises and negotiates agreements with other industry bodies where necessary. Set up the BRIT School for Performing Arts and Technology.

Concert Merchandisers' Association
199 Queen's Crescent
London NW5 4DS
Tel: 0171 485 3333
Fax: 0171 485 9986

Represents merchandising companies and lobbies venues and artists' management on issues relating to sales of merchandising at concert venues.

Millward Brown Market Research Ltd
Olympus Avenue
Tachbrook Park
Warwick CV34 6RJ
Tel: 01926 452233
Fax: 01926 833600

Compilers of the official UK charts as broadcast on the BBC and printed in a number of publications including *Music Week*. Labels must register with Millward Brown for chart eligibility. Gallup was responsible for the provision of chart information for the BBC and a range of UK publications for 10 years until Millward Brown took over from the end of January 1994.

MRIB
22 Brook Mews North
London W2 3BW
Tel: 0171 262 5797
Fax: 0171 262 5766

Compilers of national charts for Teletext UK and a range of

music publications.

National Discography (ND)
Elgar House
41 Streatham High Road
Streatham
London SW16 1ER
Tel: 0181 677 9110
Fax: 0181 664 7163

Database of all currently available commercial recordings, with details of writers, artists, publishers, labels and formats. Access to the system is available by CD-ROM or ON-LINE. Developed by MCPS.

REPRO – Guild of Recording Producers, Directors and Engineers
68 Cleveland Gardens
London SW13 0AH
Tel: 0181 876 3411
Fax: 0181 876 3411

Previously known as the British Record Producers' Guild, this is a trade association and a division of the Association of Professional Recording Services (APRS).

Scottish Music Industry Association (SMIA)
PO Box 516
Glasgow G5 8PZ
Tel: 0141 429 4174
Fax: 0141 420 1892

The SMIA aims to be the vehicle for promoting global interest in all forms of music created in Scotland, resulting in industry and public awareness of Scottish talent.

The Umbrella Organization
PO Box 763
London SE24 9LL
Tel: 0181 960-1871
Fax: 0181 969-1694

Association of independent record companies. Provides an influential voice for the independent sector. Lobbies for the best deals possible for members in areas such as formation of charts, relationships with other industry bodies and disseminating relevant information.

LEGAL

For information about courses and firms and individuals specializing in copyright law and other areas of the law which relate specifically to the music business, contact:

The Law Society
13 Chancery Lane
London WC2A 1PL
Tel: 071 242 1222
Fax: 0171 831 0344

RECORD COMPANIES

There are over 2000 record companies and labels in the UK, with many more opening up, changing names and closing down, month by month. Here we list the UK's top seven major record companies and their affiliated labels.

BMG
(including labels RCA, Arista and Deconstruction)
Bedford House
69–79 Fulham High Street
London SW6 3JW
Tel: 0171 973 0980
Fax: 0171 371 9571

EMI Records
(including labels Chrysalis, Parlophone, Capitol, IRS, EMI UK, Blue Note, Positiva and Liberty)
20 Manchester Square
London W1A 1ES
Tel: 0171 486 4488
Fax: 0171 465 0070

In 1995 EMI Records is movng to
Glacier House
44 Brook Green
London W6 7BT
Tel: 0171 603 1435

MCA Records
(including Geffen Records)
139 Piccadilly
London W1V OAX
Tel: 0171 957 8667
Fax: 0171 465 0070

PolyGram International
(including labels Decca, Philips, Deutsche Grammophon,
London, Phonogram, Polydor, Island, Wild Card and A&M)
1 Sussex Place
London W6 9SX
Tel: 0181 910 5000
Fax: 0181 741 4901

Sony Music Entertainment
(including labels Columbia, Epic and Sony Soho Square)
10 Great Marlborough Street
London W1V 2LP
Tel: 0171 911 8200
Fax: 0171 911 8600

Virgin Records
Kensal House
553–579 Harrow Road
London W10 4RH
Tel: 0171 964 6000
Fax: 0171 964 4649

WEA
28 Kensington Church Street
London W8 4EP
Tel: 0171 937 8844
Fax: 0171 938 3901

Warner's record divisions are East West and WEA Records, which together include labels Anxious, Atlantic, Allegro, Blanco Y Negro, East West, Paisley Park, Sire, Reprise, Interscope, QWest and ZTT.

• A comprehensive list of record companies operating in the UK can be found in the *Music Week Directory.* Billed as *The Comprehensive Guide to the Music Industry and Associated Service Industries,* this publication lists pretty well every music business organization in the UK, from publishers to promoters, from merchandisers to managers. Available from: Computer Postings, 120–126 Lavender Ave., Mitcham, Surrey CR4 3HP, for £30 plus £2 p&p–Tel: 0181 640 8142; or ask at your local library.

MUSIC PRESS

Trade

Applause
Applause Publications
132 Liverpool Road
London N1 1LA
Tel: 0171 700 0248
Fax: 0171 700 0301

Billboard
23 Ridgmount Street
London WC1E 7AH
Tel: 0171 323 6688
Fax: 0171 323 2314

Broadcast
EMAP Publishing
33–39 Bowling Green Lane
London EC1R ODA
Tel: 0171 837 1212
Fax: 0171 837 8250

Music & Media
23 Ridgmount Street
London WC1E 7AH
Tel: 0171 323 6686
Fax: 0171 323 2341

Music Week
Spotlight Publications
Ludgate House
245 Blackfriars Road
London SE1 9UR
Tel: 0171 620 3636
Fax; 0171 401 8035

Music Business International
Spotlight Publications
Ludgate House
245 Blackfriars Road
London SE1 9UR
Tel: 0171 620 3636
Fax: 0171 921 5984

The Stage
(incorporating Television Today)
47 Bermondsey Street
London SE1 3XT
Tel: 0171 403 1818
Fax: 0171 403 0480

Consumer

Blues & Soul
153 Praed Street
London W2 1RL
Tel: 0171 402 6869
Fax: 0171 224 8227

Kerrang!
EMAP Metro
5th Floor
Mappin House
4 Winsley Street
London WC1N 7AR
Tel: 0171 436 1515
Fax: 0171 323 0276

Melody Maker
IPC Magazines
Kings Reach Tower
Stamford Street
London SE1 9LS
Tel: 0171 261 5504
Fax: 0171 261 6706

Mojo
EMAP Metro
5th Floor
Mappin House
4 Winsley Street
London WC1N 7AR
Tel: 0171 436 1515
Fax: 0171 637 4925

New Musical Express
IPC Magazines
Kings Reach Tower
Stamford Street
London SE1 9LS
Tel: 0171 261 5519
Fax: 0171 261 5504

Q
EMAP Metro
5th Floor
Mappin House
4 Winsley Street
London WC1N 7AR
Tel: 0171 436 1515
Fax: 0171 631 0781

Smash Hits
EMAP Metro
52–55 Carnaby Street
London W1V 1PF
Tel: 0171 437 8050
Fax: 0171 494 0851

Vox
IPC Magazines
Kings Reach Tower
Stamford Street
London SE1 9LS
Tel: 0171 261 5643
Fax: 0171 261 5504

Appendix B

Music industry courses in the UK

The British Record Industry Trust (BRIT)
Performing Arts and Technology School
East Wing
Selhurst Tertiary Centre
The Crescent
Selhurst CR9 2LY
Tel: 0181 665 5242

GCSE and A-level music; music theory and instruments; Foundation Course in Performing Arts leading to BTEC in Performing Arts; BTEC National Diploma Performing Arts (Music). Recording techniques and music technology are options within the course. Some music business included with guest speakers from the industry.

Newark & Sherwood College
Friary Road
Newark NG24 1PB
Tel: 01636 705921

BTEC National Diploma in Music Industry Studies; BTEC Certificate in Music Industry Management.

Music Business Training Ltd
Unit G
44 St Pauls Crescent
Camden
London NW1 9TN
Tel: 0171 485 7412

Music business courses aimed at those people who are keen to set up businesses from scratch. Course covers all areas of the business, performance, publishing, touring, marketing, publicity, cashflows, business forecasts. Includes speakers from the music industry.

The Centre for Continuing Education
The City University
Northampton Square
London EC1V 0HB
Tel: 0171 477 8259

Offers distance learning courses including An Introduction to the Music Industry, and Planning and Developing a Music Business Project. Both the above offer feedback from music industry professionals, telephone and postal advice services and access to the Making Music Work student network.

West Lothian College
Margerybank Street
Bathgate
West Lothian EH48 1QJ
Tel: 01506 634300

HNC in Music Business Administration. Based on the Business Administration HNC with a strong element of Music Management. The course has a record label and students find a band, release and market a single. Guest speakers from all areas of the music business.

Community Education Lewisham HQ
Mornington Centre
Mornington Road
London SE8 4BL
Tel: 0181 690 0596

Music Industry Course focusing on record deals and contracts within the music industry.

City & Guilds of London Institute
46 Britannia Street
London WC1X 9RG
Tel: 0171 278 2468

Certificate in (general) Retail Distribution Skills including customer contact skills, product knowledge skills, sales support skills, merchandising, stock control, security, rights and responsibilities.

Haringey Arts Council
North Block
Selby Centre
Selby Street
Tottenham
London N17 8JN
Tel: 0181 801 9520

Music business training and sound engineering courses for the unemployed.

Kidderminster College
Hoo Road
Worcester DY10 1LX
Tel: 01562 8208

BTEC National Diploma in Performing Arts. Wide range of options from jazz and rock workshops to music business lectures and introduction to studio techniques. Guest speakers and placements in many areas of the music business.

Newcastle College
School of Performing Arts
Rye Hill
Newcastle upon Tyne NE4 7SA
Tel: 0191 273 8866

BTEC National Diploma in Popular Music. Emphasis on performance of popular music includes instrumental and group playing skills, recording, music technology, business practice and marketing studies. Professional Diploma in Music aims at the development of a high level of performance skills plus a wide variety of options including business studies. Strong emphasis on music technology and production. BTEC HND Higher National Level in Jazz, Popular and Commercial Music. Graduate Diploma in Jazz, Popular and Commercial Music.

West London Institute of Higher Education
Gordon House
300 St Margarets Road
Twickenham TW1 1PT
Tel: 0181 891 0121

Foundation Course in Performing Arts. Performance-based course training for young classical and pop/rock musicians includes reading music, recording, performance techniques and music business.

Salford College of Technology
Music Department
Adelphi Building
Peru Street
Salford
Greater Manchester M3 6EQ
Tel: 0161 834 6633

BA Hons Pop music/recording. Popular music emphasis on music technology. Good relationship with industry professionals.

Trinity College of Music
11–13 Madeville Place
London W1M 6AQ
Tel: 0171 935 5773

Degree course in musical performance, validated by the University of Westminster with vocational options including media studies, communications and teaching skills, musical directorship, music management and administration, music publishing, music librarianship and music therapy.

Colchester Institute
School of Music
Sheepen Road
Colchester CO3 3LL
Tel: 01206 761660

A-Level and degree foundation courses.

The Rockschool Ltd.
Broomfield House
10 Broomfield Road
Richmond TW9 3HS
Tel: 0181 332 6303

The examining body for the only unified system of rock guitar, bass and drums tuition in the world – approved by the Trinity College of Music.

Greenwich Community College
Rosemary Hill
Corelli Road
London SE3 8EP
Tel: 0181 319 8088

Making It In The Music Business. Four courses: musicianship; performance; recording; marketing and promotion.

Guildhall School of Music
Barbican
London ECY 8DT
Tel: 0171 628 2571

Courses and workshops in performance, recording and engineering.

Hackney Community College
Keltan House
89–115 Mare Street
London E8 4RG
Tel: 0181 533 5922

BTEC National Diploma in Performing Arts and adult education courses in jazz performance.

Bath College of Higher Education
Newton Park
Newton St Loe
Bath
Avon BA2 9BN
Tel: 01225 873701

BA Hons degrees in music and the relative arts.

Chicester College of Technology
Westgate Fields
Chichester PO19 1SB
Tel: 01243 786321

BTEC National Diploma in Popular Music.

South East Derbyshire College
Field Road
Ilkeston DE7 5RS
Tel: 0115 932 4212

BTEC in the performing arts with jazz options and GCSE and A-level music courses.

Harlow College
East Site
The Hides
Harlow CM20 3RA
Tel: 01279 441288

BTEC First Diploma in Performing Arts and BTEC National Diploma in Popular Music.

City of Leeds College of Music
Cokridge Street
Leeds LS2 8BH
Tel: 0113 243 2391

Composers and songwriters courses; pop, rock and jazz piano; pop rock and jazz group playing; A-level music; Graduate Diploma in Jazz and Contemporary Music.

Wakefield District College
Margaret Street
Wakefield WF1 2DH
Tel: 01924 810234

BTEC National Diploma in Popular Music.

National Council for the Training of Journalists
The Latton Bush Centre
Southern Way
Harlow CM18 7BL
Tel: 01279 430009

Basic journalistic training with hands-on experience and later specialization.

Index

Page numbers appearing in *italics* refer to addresses and brief descriptions in the appendices.